7 Mar 2009

To Kay,
my Grange mentor.
No amount of words can thank
you for the support throughout
the years.
Love & Peace,
Laura R. Combs

Life After Traumatic Experience

Beating the Odds

Laura R. Combs

authorHOUSE®

AuthorHouse™
1663 Liberty Drive, Suite 200
Bloomington, IN 47403
www.authorhouse.com
Phone: 1-800-839-8640

© 2008 Laura R. Combs. All rights reserved.

No part of this book may be reproduced, stored in a retrieval system, or transmitted by any means without the written permission of the author.

First published by AuthorHouse 2/25/2008

ISBN: 978-1-4343-6214-8 (sc)

Library of Congress Control Number: 2008900785

Printed in the United States of America
Bloomington, Indiana

This book is printed on acid-free paper.

Disclaimer: The issues in this book could trigger strong feelings and emotions. If you have trouble coping with your emotions, please speak with a professional, and be good to yourself. Many emotions were triggered putting this book together. I had to continually remind myself the memories can't hurt you in themselves, it's what we do with them, and how we perceive the situations we were in. Asking for help shows strength and courage and is in no way a sign of weakness. If anyone tells you otherwise, that person needs their head examined.

This Book Is Dedicated To:

All those who have had a Near-Death Experience and don't know where to share it. Marge Lord Church and her Mother, Lillian for their continued courage in physical struggles and how they overcome their hardships. You have been an inspiration to me.

To Sylvia Klien Oklin, for all her encouragement, putting the twins' story in her book, and may She be at peace with the Lord of our Universe. Deepest sympathies to Her husband Bob, and children.

To my Aunt Adeline, I understand the pain you have been going through all these years. It's not the regular physical pain that one would think you go through from an auto accident, but the nerve pain can almost drive you into insanity, because soft tissue damage doesn't show up on x-rays or any other scan made to assist doctors in their diagnoses.

And Most of All, To my husband, Dave who stuck it out with me through thick and thin, not knowing what would happen next, and just loving and supporting me. Dave's trust has been tested to" The Max! ", and I Thank him for sticking with me through the hard difficult times.

Contents

Acknowledgements		xi
Foreword By Dr. Christopher Bentley		xix
1	The Near Death Experience	1
2	Tunnel Knowledge?	5
3	Life Turned Upside Down & Sideways	9
4	Time Loss and Multiple Personality Disorder	13
5	Vision Techniques: With Dr. Susan C. Danberg	22
6	Resolving Conflict (Past & Present)	24
7	Learning How to Open Up & Trust	31
8	A Loving Tribute to My Mom	35
9	An Experience with DCF in Our Lives	37
10	Memory Recall: (U.S. Army) Tour of Duty	41
11	Near-death Experiences and Common Side Effects	58
12	Going to the Light After the Twins Were Born	64
13	Another Story of a Near-death Experience "A Second Chance", By Mrs. Jennifer L. Babb Davis	66
14	Spiritual Recovery & Making Peace Hanging's	74
15	Stories from Others	82
16	A Warning About the Dark Side: Intrigue & Mystery	87
17	Head-on Crash * No Where to Go *	103
18	The Mountain Climb that Turned into a Nightmare	105
19	The Mistake on Mt. Crawford By Lee R. Combs	110
20	The Music that Has Inspired Me & Suggested Readings for Better Understanding	112

Acknowledgements

To my parents and my brothers for the support, that the trials and tribulations of life didn't break us apart, and that our lives have come full circle to who we are today. Thank you for your love, support, and encouragement.

To Dave, my husband and twin sons, Lee & Keith. You have filled me with the best joy that life has to offer. You have made all my dreams a reality beyond words.

To my ex-sister-in-law, Jennifer L. Babb Davis, who will be sharing her own near-death experience in a later chapter. Thank you for all your encouragement and support with this book.

To Elizabeth Monahan and Dr. Eva Salzer, for helping me get back in touch with my body and my emotions. And for the third time around. These two having never given up on me or allowing me to give up on myself. You have given me the courage to feel the pain, show the anger, and frustration that goes with chronic pain. Thank You.

To Charity, for all that you did for me with my first accident in '89, you helped me organize my time, and listened to me through some real difficult times. Thank You. Wishing you the best in all your future endeavors.

To Michelle for listening when things were really hard to deal with, you gave me a lot of encouragement, strength, and support. Best Wishes in all your future Endeavors. Thank you for just being there.

To Dr. Susan C. Danberg, for helping me correct my vision, not just in a physical sense, but in a visual, spiritual, and emotional sense.

To Theresa, Dr. Danberg's former receptionist, for by example, her strong faith in God by what has happened in her own life, and the struggles thereof. And to Wilma, for her encouragement and strength. Thank You.

To Marge Lord Church, a friend I grew up with and shared many of my dreams. Marge believed I would accomplish everything I set out to do, despite the obstacles. Thank You for your support and encouragement. Marge and I both had speech problems growing up and have overcome that problem, unless we are under a lot of stress and upset. Marge has been an inspiration to me, her Mother too, because of their severe arthritis complications thereof, and when I had doctors' appointments. I couldn't have accomplished all I did without your help.

To Virginia, for taking me to doctor appointments and helping me out when my car has left me stranded on the road side, when I couldn't drive myself to appointments, and to Bob Jr. who also helped by taking care of the boys while I had appointments, and I could not have done all that I have if they were not here. Peace to you always.

To my Aunt Stasia, who with Her help in babysitting while I went to doctor appointments, it helped me more than you'll ever know, and be at peace always.

To Colleen, Lisa, Lynn, Nancy, Ginny, Reverie, Karen, Debbie, Pat, Kathy, June, John, Smokey, Len, David, Thom, Pete, Becky, Wendy, and everyone else in rooms of a Recovery Program I have been in contact with. Thank You.

To Marilyn, John, and Kristen Planny, for all your support and counsel during and after High School.

To Mrs. Nancy Paladino for all her help and support in High School and the books she used to read to us. Thank You for the extra encouragement while I was in your Special Ed Class you taught. The book Mrs. Mike is the only book I can remember that you read to us Special Ed Students, and the book that I had kept in my heart to get through some of my toughest problems. It has given me much courage and strength. God be with you wherever you are.

To Donna Doube' Hyrb , for her counsel and help with a recovery program, for supporting me in my research efforts to find out more about myself, and for the Women's Group she affiliates at the Hartford Vet Center.

The Staff of the Marlborough Family Practice in Connecticut. Dr. Bentley has given me many opportunities to share with him, learn to trust that the medical system can be trusted, that honesty is important, and humility to conform to medical treatment is safe. (Not always pleasant, but Safe!). To further the research studies to come and those under-way. And a Big Thank You to all the other Doctors, Nurses, and Clerical Staff who listened to me during some real trying times.

To Rhonda & Rod Lane, for the help in my research and using their prodigy, the long time we spend on the phone and after IANDS Support Group Meetings at Murphy & Scarlette's. Or for just listening and being supportive. Best Wishes for your book. Also the connection we have on the computer, support, and encouragement!

To Alexandra Tegius, for her class on Death, Grief, and Loss. I really got a lot of understanding of my own Near-Death Experience from that class. Thank You.

To Nancy Evans Bush & Leslee Morabito, for helping me understand my own NDE.

To Bruce Greyson for helping me with some mental support, Diane Mann, Donna, Jack, Martha, and Nancy Kruger for help on Multiple Personality issues.

To Jack Lardis, your Art work is excellent, the depth in which you paint is very deep into yourself, your suggestions on the work I have done in the past is well taken, and to learn how to sell my work to the public hasn't been one of my strong points. All the art work I have done so far has gone to charity. The money raised has been given to The Diabetes's Association, Kidney Associations, Cancer Research, and other numerous Charities. I do Thank You for your help.

To Sandra and Ned for the loving support at the IANDS Conference when I spoke for the first time in a public setting. Thank You.

To Anneliese Fox, for her help with the IANDS Conference, Research, and being a Special Support Person on Near-Death issues.

To my Cousin Carol Angell, for watching the twins so I could go to doctor appointments, support groups, or to just have some time alone. And most of all, for always being there. Rest in Peace.

To Sandra Lucas, for her Mandala to focus on during pregnancy, labor, and delivery of the twins, and connecting me with the Author of the Positive Pregnancy Fitness Book, Sylvia Klein Oklin. Thank You Both for the encouragement of this book.

To Linda Ravenell for helping baby-sit during hospital appointments, just being a dear friend, and comrade. I hope Hawaii is a better environment for you.

To Terry and Mike for helping me out when times were tough, when the gallstones were acting up and for just listening to me. Terry is also my physic twin, ever since we met. Terry has always been here with us when we have needed someone to care for the twins, and for being that loving person that you are. Best of Luck in all your future Endeavors.

To all those at Quality Name Plate who allowed me to share my experiences with them and trained me in the few jobs I did. To Debbie, Mary, Vada, Bruce, Pat, Tim, John, Mike, Chad, Jeff, Ann, Carolyn, Cliff, Arron, Amos, Edith, Gary, Craig, Rai-Ann, Lorraine, and Terry. To Bernie Dennler, and Paul & Craig Garneau for giving me a job and letting me stay when I was experiencing some personality problems. Thank you for the opportunities in working with you. All the Best in your Future Endeavors.

To Jeanette, I'll always remember you, you spoke your mind and left nothing to question, you helped me a great deal, and your love for music touched my heart. Good Luck in Whatever your Endeavors may be.

To Vicky, you stuck it out with me in group, I hope all is well with you and your family, and Wish you the Best with your Journey in this Life.

To Dr. Amy E. Charney, you helped me a great deal in the time we worked together on family & Service Issues. It ended on a sad heart, but I was encouraged to continue at a different time.

To Pam & Harry Williams, for all your love, support, and friendship. You are very special to me and that you have helped me many times to pick up the pieces when life got too difficult. I hope we get reconnected down the road. I miss You.

To Vi Schwarzman, for all the help you have given me or members of my family. Thank You for Being There.

To Fred & Valerie Hill Baker, for being the Godparents of our twin sons, for listening, for the comfort, and support. The editing for this book has been done by Valerie. Thank You.

To Patricia Moon for continued support and care given during some real hard times. Thank You.

To Claudia Wolf-Davey, Thank You for the courage to take back control of my life and become grounded in who I really am. I really hated the way you left, I can only hope that things are right with you and your children. Best of Luck, Wherever you are?

To Dr. Sarah J. Gamble, for helping me stay in the here and now, for the courage to express the pain, frustration, and anger. And for helping me with the Military & Social issues. And your professional insight with this book.

To Dr. Sandra Hartiagen, for your continued support when I was first trying to get professional help in my life, (back in civilian life after spending sometime in the U.S. ARMY), you really helped me learn to trust, although, our time together was short, you gave me the courage, and confidence to continue on my own.

To John & Nancy Valentine, the rest of the Marlborough Florist Staff, Thank You for all the support you have given me, and my family. For the extra flowers, love, care, support, and selling my Peace Hangings, so to give the money to charities, and just being there. You probably don't know how much you have helped me. Thank You.

To my cousin Kathy, Brain, and Karen. Thank You for all that you have helped me with, you have given me much inspiration for all that you have been through, and have taught me many things that have been a great encouragement. God Bless you all.

To Pastor Miesel, Amy, and all connected with Bethlehem Lutheran Church, Thank You for your continued support, love, and care. Thank You.

To John Ducheon, I have gotten back my spiritually, it has taken a too long time, I just didn't bounce back as well from that last Traumatic incident with the Cement Truck. I know that you have been concerned, it has just taken a while to get back in a writing posture.

To Betty Goldstein, Becky Wynn, Ann Corbett, Pat, Kathy Othon, Smitty, Sgt. Smith, Sgt.Burnett, SP4 Carlson, Sgt. Washington, Lt. Candlemire, Marge, Ellen, Munchkin, Sharon, Col. Little, and those who were not specifically mentioned from my Tour of Duty in Panama, Thank You for being there, and you all really helped save my life.

To Larry & Linda Ingalls, Paul & Rachel Paulson, Terry & Lori Enfalt, The Ball Family, Yolanda, Louis, Susan, Rita and Family, Richard, John Fisher, Leo, and all others who were involved with the Oversees Christian Service Centers In Panama. Thank you for God's intervention in my Life down in Panama.

To the Cuna Indian Tribe in the Darien, thank you for the wonderful experience of your healing powers, and knowing the God of our Universe. You all taught me more about God than anyone will ever know. Thank You. Mucho Gracias'.

To the Taxi driver who helped me out of many bad situations, you were always there when I was in some kind of trouble. Thank You.

To Robin Grant-Hall, you have helped renew my faith in the therapy department, and working on many issues of my life, you have helped to keep me structured, present, and helping to sort out some of the major issues pertaining to my Tour of Duty in the U.S. ARMY. Thank You for Being There.

To My Mom, you have showed me much strength, and courage. You are a warrior, Peace Maker, and a loving devoted Mother and Grandmother. Most of all, you are my best friend, and full of inspiration. Thank You for being You.

To Tracy Gibson and Yadirah, and all the parents in the parenting classes I attended, Thank You for your continued support and care.

To Dr. Bernice Szafarek, Kim, and Staff, Thank you for all your help, support, care for me, and my family. For encouraging me to take care of my dental needs, that of my Husband, and Twins. Thank You for getting me more involved with raising funds for Cancer Research.

To God for this life I have experienced, you gave me life, the greatest gift of all, and in return is my gift to You. The people you have put in my life, for as short or as long as they were allowed, and for the guidance of others not mentioned. Thank You.

To Professor Glynn Owens for all your help from New Zealand, a few of your students essays and just being a caring person.

To Devon Stallard, for his story. God Speed to you and your family.

To all at The Columbia Congregational Church for who my Family belongs. Thank You for the support and encouragement.

To our new Choir Director who has been a support in trying new ventures, like the bell choir, and learning to use musical instruments during our music ministry.

To Rev. Robert G. Woodward, Thank You for all the spiritual support and encouragement.

To Anne Robinson for all your help and letting me help volunteer in the office. It was a great learning experience and helped me connect with the goings on in the church. It also, helped me feel a part of the church family.

To Anne B. Lewis, my pen pal out of California. You really helped encourage me to get this book finished. I pray for you in all your New Endeavors!

To Carol, Janice, Rebecca, Su Epstein and the rest of the Staff at the Saxton B. Free Library in Columbia, CT. Thank You for your support and expertise.

To all who weren't specifically mentioned. Thank You, God Bless You, and Peace to You Always.

Foreword

By Dr. Christopher Bentley

I was extremely flattered to have been asked to write a foreword for Laura's book. When she first told me of her idea, I thought that it was a great way for her to look back and summarize what she had gone through and how much she had learned. After the warm glow of being honored wore off however, I wondered, why me?

I've known Laura for a long time. She was probably one of my first patients when I joined our practice 20 years ago. I reflected on our interactions and what prompted her to ask me. The answer did not come easy.

Then I read her book. It was only then that I realized what Laura truly had gone through and why she needed this book. It is not a summary of her experience but a story of endurance and strength.

Upon first reading, you get a feel that the book is disjointed and sometimes difficult to follow. This is not an accident or a flaw. Rather, it is a wonderful portrayal of what life for Laura was like. There were many times when she left my office that I had no idea what the heck just happened. At times I felt I was talking to a stranger. Sometimes

I wondered if it was Laura or me, but I was sure that one of us was on a different page. Sometimes angry, sometimes boisterous, sometimes jovial, and sometimes too faimiliar, these visits were difficult to summarize when I went to dictate my note.

What struck me was how often Laura mentions me in the book. In a life that must have been chaotic and confusing, Laura refers back to our visits frequently. And there were many visits. We talked about so many things that were happening in her life, the difficult times as well as the joyous times. The loss of her father. Her marriage to Dave. The birth of her two wonderful sons.

At first, I was disturbed by how Laura portrayed me. I'd like to have been remembered for intelligent diagnoses or remarkable insight. Instead, I really was more of a sounding board and my medical record really does reflect this. I was living this and learning along with Laura. Far from the sage advisor, I was becoming a caring friend.

Then it struck me. This was a journey that Laura was on. A long hard road to discover herself and heal many scars, both physical and emotional. Maybe she didn't need a sage advisor as much as she needed a supporter who she could turn to for comfort. Maybe she needed someone who believed in her, who had experienced these things with her. She needed someone who could assure her that she was doing a great job navigating through difficult times that most people never have to go.

This book is a story of survival. It is Laura's chronicle of the difficult times that she endured and the struggle to recover her life and her family. I'm proud to be considered a part of it. I have certainly learned a great deal. I'm thankful for the lessons I've learned. I did believe that Laura would turn out all right even, at times, when she didn't. That was my job, small as it was.

Maybe that's a larger part of my job than I realized. With all the emphasis these days on performance and getting patients to goal, a basic part of medicine has been forgotten-compassion. In the words of Edward Trudeau, the founder of a renowned tuberculosis sanatorium in the 1800's, "To cure sometimes to relieve often, to comfort always." A good lesson for all family physicians. Thank you Laura.

1

The Near Death Experience

Vehicle 1 was traveling East Bound on Route 66, Vehicle 1, driven by a white Caucasian female, was struck by Vehicle 2, driven by a white Caucasian male. Vehicle 1, was a white VW Golf, and Vehicle 2, was a Ford heavy duty truck with a plow on the front.

Time of accident was 8:08 pm on this day of Sunday, April 16, 1989. The driver of the VW Golf was seriously injured and transported to Hartford Hospital by request because she had a head injury. Vehicle 2 was issued a summons for failing to heed the traffic light. Vehicle 2 was heading South Bound on Main Street before striking Vehicle 1 broad sided.

This is the type of statement you would find on a police report. The time between getting struck by the truck and the paramedics arriving was what seemed like hours. Almost like time stopped or continued on a different level. I was told it was only minutes, but from what condition I was in, it didn't feel that way.

I felt strange after the accident, I heard the other driver say, " I am getting help!", and then everything went totally black. I could see all these stars around me, it was eerie, yet I wasn't afraid, and I felt extremely warm and peaceful. I was in this purplish, transparent tunnel, and I could still see all the stars in the sky, only there were no stars out that evening, because of the rain. I ran to the light in this tunnel, but I was only about nine years old, not twenty-six the age I was when the accident occurred. There was water up to the calf of my legs. I had never recalled feeling so loved as I did in this tunnel.

I ran towards the light, no fear, no pain, just curiosity, and telepathic information that came so fast that I had no time to interpret. I heard a voice of a man telling me, "I had to go back, because it wasn't my time!",and that the information given would come back, but not quickly, and He has been right so far. Before I got to the light I was sent back to my body. When I came too, the first words I spoke were "Oh, F---, I was sent back!". One of the paramedics was a bit taken back by the language, but that is how it was, or at least my perception of it. I still felt different, like I no longer belonged on this planet, and this really scared me into silence, because I was afraid I would be committed to a rubber room if I spoke about this experience.

I was real angry about the situation, but it didn't end there, because I told the paramedics how to get me out of my car without using the jaws-of-life, I guess they figured I was fine. Actually, I didn't want to hear the metal cutting off my door, because I felt my head would explode, because of the loud noise it would make. The Staff at Hartford Hospital didn't keep me for observation with the head injury I had sustained, that the wound was superficial. Not quite the answer to the problem. Actually, the migraines lasted over four years. I still get them, but very rarely. There was also this severe chemical in balance that needed some attention.

If the accident wasn't traumatizing enough, get a load of what happened the next day, the Police Officer at the scene of the accident called to give his sympathies and I answered the phone, and what a shock to hear I wasn't expected to live. I was real upset and hung up the phone. I didn't know what to do with that information and said nothing to anyone about it. (To be honest, I forgot the whole conversation had taken place).

The first year was sheer Hell. I had visions of things to come and visions of things that happened in other states and countries. (Past and Present Events)

Relationships I had didn't last up to this point. At work, there was a 40th Anniversary Dinner, and I needed a date. My Mother's best friend has a son, and I called him for a date. We went out a week before the Anniversary, just in case we didn't get along, I could find someone else. We went out and found we had a lot in common and really liked each other. I thought to myself when he came to the door, this man is real cute, and has a great sense of humor. I knew a lot about him without him telling me, because I found out that he was my school friend's boyfriend before she moved away to the west coast. I let Dave tell me about himself, because I didn't want to give myself away like that. Only to both of us, I did give away the knowledge of what I knew and much more as our relationship evolved, and we got married a few years later.

Backing up a bit, the Fall of 1989, I decided to go to college, and was that a great experience for me, except I began to lose time, and that led to a lot of mistrust. I couldn't account for my whereabouts at times. The migraines got real bad that I was having trouble at work. It took my co-workers six months before they finally spoke up and brought the problems I was having to my attention. I was still having trouble, but people at work helped out where they could. The accident case was still pending a trial date. There wasn't much support, the problems didn't cease. After three years, a dead grandma, and much confusion, my supervisor called me into the office. We have a job on the other side of the company we would like you to try, it was low stress, and maybe I could get the help I needed.

First, we got the eyes checked, found out through testing that I had a traumatic brain injury, that what I was experiencing was residuals of that head injury from the accident. The rest the doctors left as a question.

In the Spring Semester at College, I took a psychology class, and Alexandra Teguis was the Professor. The class was on Death, Grief, and Loss. I aced that class by the way. I threw myself into research and it was fun, it was also a major learning experience for me. Nancy Evans Bush and Leslee Morabito spoke to the class on Near-Death Studies. Nancy was the President of IANDS, at the time, which is the International Association on Near-Death Studies. This class was different, the energy was astronomical beyond belief. The events of this night changed my life, my ideas, my spiritual being became acutely aware of what had happened that rainy night a year before, and without question. It took a couple more years and a psychological evaluation at the Newington VA Hospital to get me to the IANDS Support Group in Farmington, at the U-CONN Medical Health Care Center, and this referral came from Dr. Cox, whom I haven't seen since, but maybe someday I can thank her in person. It was brought to my attention that IANDS doesn't have a support group, that it's a meeting for "Friends of IANDS", but to me it has made a world of difference in how I live my life today. (Support Group or Not!). I guess I knew deep down inside me that maybe a book would come out of this experience, that maybe, if one person could be helped by this book, that it would be worth everything that was put into it.

I share my experience, because as it was written in the Bible, we are supposed to help one another, and not hurt one another. This is not a power or control issue, it's based on love, courage, hope, peace, respect, and trust.

I have taken the resources I have needed to survive, I want to help others who may be suffering from any trauma, that everyone's mission in this life is different, to respect others, and you may receive the same respect back. (Not Always)

The rest of the chapters in this book will differ in length, depending on material, topic, and experience.

2

Tunnel Knowledge?

First of all, What is Tunnel Knowledge? and how does it apply to the present time? I believe that tunnel knowledge is Godly. How it applies to the present time? It does and it doesn't. Doctors and Psychiatrists are stating it has something to do with the lack of oxygen that makes the tunnel effect and they're just making an educated guess at that. No two NDE's (Near Death Experiences are the same). I feel that NDE's are more subjective, not objective.

Although, Dr. Susan Blackmore may have a difference of opinion, based on her own research, and NDE). There are things that science will never be able to explain, that is part of the mystery of life, and this is just fine with me. Others may feel differently and that's okay too.

In my research, not all NDE's have a tunnel to speak of, others have a scene of paradise, and others are in a blissful state. There are such NDE's that are hellish, but I will discuss that in a later chapter.

To help you understand tunnel knowledge and give it some clarity, tunnel knowledge is based on a different time and space environment, and I believe the information that is given is boundless, is without limit, that space, time, and matter is unconditional in nature.

This is only my opinion, it may or may not be agreed upon by others. I feel that the information I received was given for me to fulfill a specific mission, that others are given information in the same manner that is specific to them. What I have learned I am sharing to the best of my ability and memory. I feel that the information I learned in the tunnel was meant to be shared to help others understand themselves and how we communicate with one another.

Even though a lot of my past had been eliminated, I get information back in fragments, and sometimes I am blessed enough to get a whole picture or story of my past. It can be quite frustrating for me and my family at times.

Several things were telepathically given: who my husband would be, that I would have twins, I could have been told the gender, but I didn't remember that, and that's okay. I did marry the man I was told about in the tunnel, I did have twins, and both of us are enjoying those two bouncy, joyful, and happy boys.

I learned I had two other NDEs while I was in the U.S. ARMY, that one was peaceful and the first was hellish. With a Traumatic Brain Injury, it is hard to say what has happened to the memories, I get some and not others. I suppose that is meant to be. There is an element about the tunnel I am still researching and it's about Time. I couldn't wear a watch for about six years or so, because I couldn't seem to keep the right time, for some reason, the time would run fast, or super slow, and I simply got tired of being late for work or appointments. Sometimes I was a day early and sometimes I didn't get where I was going at all.

Now that I am a Mom, it was agreed upon that I stay home, that if the money situation deems me to go back to work, I would go. I am not a slacker, shammer (Slang for not doing your work), or lazy, on the contrary, as a Mom, and I am quite busy. I can say, that when I worked, I really enjoyed the job, and the opportunities I was given. It never ceases to amaze me, what I learn from the twins, and that everything we do is good enough.

That we will never be perfect, I believe that is God's job, that as long as we are doing our best, and you know what is best and so does God. To me, it's God; to you out there, it's who you call your Higher

Power. It's not for me to say. I feel that religion is a personal choice and a private expression.

I feel by writing this book, it brings me to a new level of self and my relationships with others. I am learning to share more of myself, get to let others know that I really do care, and that I am not that hard to get along with. I may, at times be hard to understand, and I do get loud at times. Those who know me can vouch that I am fairly harmless. If provoked, that's another story, and I would rather not write about it. Let's just safely say, "This is just one of my character defects!" and leave it at that.

Before I get to chapter three, I have to say that it has been the toughest chapter to get through, thus far, and personally challenging. I had another accident, but it happened while I was writing chapter three, and it put me in such a void, I didn't know how I would get out. With much professional and family support, and with courage I feel that I can overcome this void.

Actually, this void has been like being in hell, with no way out, and I felt so alone. I took one of my therapist's suggestions to include her, Dave, the twins, and anyone else I would feel comfortable having in the void. That the most important thing is that I don't be alone, and that I share these feelings and not keep them to myself. (No matter how uncomfortable I feel!) Keeping the feelings to myself, not sharing them are the makings of a dangerous situation, and I don't feel comfortable taking that kind of risk.

It was scary to let someone in on the pain I was feeling, not just physically, but emotionally, and spiritually. I was angry, scared, sad, mad, frustrated, feeling guilty, hateful, alone, unsupported, unforgiving, helpless, and just totally twigged out.

In conclusion, I am working to put some closure on some of my accident anniversaries. There is life after traumatic experience, it isn't an easy journey, but it can be easier if you don't shut people out of your life who you are close to.

A Gentle Warning: Don't assume anything, no one else is going to understand what you are going through, unless they've been there themselves, yet, let others know what is happening with you, and don't keep explaining yourself.

Suggested Readings

My Cousin Mary sent me the book CREATIVE RELAXATION Turning Your Stress Into Positive Energy by Dr. Deborah Bright. It was a big help.

While I was attending College at MCC in Manchester, CT, I took a class on Death, Grief, and Loss. I met Elisabeth Kubler-Ross's Under Study Student Alexandria Tegis. That is when I first started reading about NDE's (Near Death Experiences), and I still am reading but writing my own experiences.

On Death and Dying

On Children and Death

Until We say "Good-Bye" all by Elizabeth Kubler-Ross, M.D.

Coming Back: A Psychiatrist Explores Past-Life Journeys by Raymond A. Moody, JR., M.D.

When Bad Things Happen To Good People by Harold S. Kushner

Saved By The Light by Dannion Brinkley with Paul Perry

To Glorify God by Nell Collins I met Her at a Church A day After a Missionary Friend was Married. Nell was speaking at her church.

And Barbara Harris, what can I say, she really helped me out a lot in the first six months I was going to the Friends of IANDS Support Group. The Book Full Circle was a big hit by then, but the Book Spiritual Awakenings: A Guidebook for Experiencer's and Those Who Care about Them really did the trick for me.

3

Life Turned Upside Down & Sideways

It was three weeks later that I got back behind any wheel of a vehicle after the accident of '89. My Mom took me out, she felt that I wouldn't drive again, and knew it was time to get back into life. I did okay, but when I drove in the center of Marlborough, it would give me the shakes, and that's why this chapter has been so hard for me. I was in another accident, my husband only waited two days, because it couldn't wait, and I had appointments with doctors and attorneys.

This brings me back to the accident of April 16, 1989. It took three weeks more to find another Volks Wagon, I figured the other had saved my life, it was only fitting that I find another, and this time I bought a VW Jetta.

Time was passing, work was not going as well as I thought, attitudes were tense, and nothing seemed to be going well. I changed chiropractors, doctors, and made myself totally exhausted. With much discussion with psychotherapist Elizabeth Monahan, she referred me to her collegue Dr. Eva Salzer, and with both their expertise I started to make some progress.

Six months after the accident, my co-worker, Pat, mentioned that I was making a lot of errors in my inspections of the silkscreen work being done, and maybe I ought to get my eyes checked. After discussing these problems with Dr. Salzer, she in turn referred me to Dr. Susan C. Danberg.

By this time, I was having trouble in my job, I had started back to college, and I was losing a lot of time. Dr. Danberg realized that I was having frequent changes in sight and that my personality wasn't always the same. I was getting a lot of headaches, and by this time I was in a relationship.

Elizabeth went as far as she could go with the therapy we were doing and would hang in there with me for more crisis intervention, if this was necessary. I was referred to the Trauamatic Stress Institute for further therapy. It took a year to finally get into a survivors group. Dr. Amy E. Charney took on the individual sessions. After I started the group, all hell broke lose. By this time I was seeing so many doctors, that my primary care physician took hold of the reins, and we started to consolidate the treatments.

Dr. Bentley was surprised about how things got so chaotic. On top of seeing all these doctors, college, work, therapy, eye training to correct vision trouble, and the list goes on, and through all of this I was losing so much more time. It was finally determined that there was a dissociative disorder going on.

It took awhile to accept that fact, but my boyfriend finally sat me down, told me some of the stuff that was happening, and convinced me that things were definitely out of hand.

Some examples are: not getting home until the wee hours of the next day with no explanation of my whereabouts, attitude and voice changes, temperament and loss of sensitivity, being abusive verbally, sometimes physically, times of just rambling off from a conversation, and it seemed like my thoughts weren't connected to my body.

I got three different opinions about what was happening, the only statement that jived with these opinions were: that I have been suffering from residuals of a Traumatic Brain Injury, that from the findings, there was very little support, and I feel that hurt the most. I felt a loss in confidence, self-esteem, and there was a big void that needed to be filled.

There were some lows and there were some big highs. I lost my paternal Gramma in Jan. of 1991. God Bless her Soul. I really have missed her. She's in a better place now.

In my work place, the employer, Mr. Garneau gave me a change in jobs, and maybe with less stress I would lose less time. I would no longer be working with Pat, Mary, Debbie, Bruce, Vada, Jim, Tim, John, Carolyn, and Mike. I did get to work with Gary, Craig, Rai-Ann, Terry, Kevin, Chad, Jeff, and Cory. I still walked with Debbie at lunch time, we would walk around the block, and then have lunch with co-workers. These walks also depended on the weather conditions.

My fiancé and I were married on June 6, 1992.

The survivors group at the Traumatic Stress Institute ended. The accident case from the April 16, 1989 was settled.

On our first Wedding Anniversary, we put a down payment for our first house. It was nice to have a place of our own, that the money that we were spending was going towards getting a deed, and we made sure we had a safe place to play, if and when we had kids?

In October of the next year, Dr. Bentley told me it was time I got back into Life, and have a family. I wasted no time in getting pregnant. Dr. Bentley was surprised I got pregnant so soon. The weekend of conception was at a Dart Tournament.

Being pregnant forced me into drug withdrawal, I couldn't take the antidepressants while I was pregnant, and that made for a real hard pregnancy. All I could take was my thyroid and the vitamins the doctor prescribed.

Between the withdrawal and hormonal changes that take place during pregnancy, I am not sure which was worse. Then with a few alter personalities still on the rampage, everything I did was questionable. Dave and I dealt with the changes accordingly. There were a few rough spots, but as long as we communicated, we did a lot of that, and everything else just fell into place by itself.

Life was like an emotional roller coaster, you didn't know from one day to the next what would happen, there was a family parent aid to make sure life for our twins was stable, and it was. Learning to communicate was essential. Some days the emotions were so strong that it was hard to stay present.

This brings us to a close in this chapter. The rest of the chapters include the information about my research with Multiple Personality Disorder and how I have integrated the others in my life. This is a sensitive area in which I am disclosing to the public. I feel there are others who are afraid to integrate, because they will lose parts of themselves they like. This in not true, integration only means that you become more whole and less fragmented.

I have been through a lot, many have been through much worse, and there is more freedom with integration. This is only based on my own experiences and some of others I have known.

Keep in mind, that life is a journey, and what happens in this journey depends on you and your Higher Power. In the Star Trek Movie Generations, Captain Picard at the end of the Movie says, " That we should Embrace Time as a Companion, that it goes with us in our Journey of Life. It's not what we leave behind that matters as much as How We Have Lived!" There was deep emotion that came with that thought, tears of joy, tears of lost time spent in a oblivion, drug & alcohol addiction, having been spared, and Given the Gift to Share the Experience of Recovery. (You're Not Cured, just Given a Reprieve.)

I have learned, you don't need a Doctor's Degree to be a Humanitarian, all you need to do is Act Humane. I believe it was Dr. Sarah J. Gamble who shared that with me, she is young, and wise.

4

Time Loss and Multiple Personality Disorder

I look back on the Time Loss, I know there is no way to make up for that time, and I go on with my life. When this Time Loss was given a name, it was a shock, and real incredible to believe at first. When I finally accepted the fact there was a dissociative disorder that was causing my Time Loss, it became a new journey to find out who I really am, and how many alter personalities there were. There were five alters besides my own.

This research has been a slow process. How much information was available?, Not very much at first.

One personality was named Southpaw, she writes left handed, didn't talk, She is about six years old, likes to doodle, and knows a little sign language. Alter No. 1 (Integrated-Yes 1998?).

Rosie. She is organized, ten years older than myself, blunt to the point, likes to listen to Classical & Irish Music, and writes left handed. She is an ex-nun. I say this, because she carries Rosary Beads with her everywhere She goes. We still carry these beads with us during times of deep distress. Alter No. 5 (Integrated-Yes 1998?).

Samantha, She is 6'5", strong southern accent, protector, wrestles with gators, good fighter, right handed, and a real southern belle. Alter No.3 Has a big Ego, (Integrated-Yes! 2007).

Cynthia, quiet, strong motives in question, right handed, organized, southern accent, liked to come out as her own separate self, and we are all happy with this. Alter No.2 (Integrated-Yes 1998?)

And lastly, there is Tinjcia, she is a character, black, fun loving, organized, knows the martial arts, loves to dance & sing in clubs, trust worthy, left handed, likes the arts, and accepts life on life's terms. Alter No. 4 (Integrated-Yes! 2006)

By the research conducted and the process of therapies I am undertaking, it is evident that these personalities had been with me a long time. That maybe Rosie was the only personality stemmed from the accident in '89. That She is to bring the truths of my past to light. To guide and help me to accept what was given to me in the tunnel. This is only a theory.

The alter personalities were very gifted to not have been detected sooner in my life. I was twenty-six when they were beginning to interfere with my daily life. A colleague of mine also had MPD (Short for Multiple Personality Disorder). After one of her speaking engagements at the college, we were discussing one of her topics, and she came out and said, "I feel that you may have MPD!", that I was different from our earlier conversation that day, (from which I didn't recall having), and I did some art work while she was speaking and I wanted to discuss it with her after her talk.

When we went for refreshments, I showed her the drawings I did during her talk, Sherry asked if she could have the pictures I drew, and I said she could when I finished the details on them. I would give them to her in our next class. (The drawings were about Sherry and her descriptions of integration.)

Sherry had 97 personalities to integrate. Sherry had only thirteen integrated when I first met her. Sherry has a home business called, "Listen to the Children!". I took all Sherry told me in the short time I knew her, worked on finding out more about MPD, and what treatments would be most affective.

Not much treatment was done, my trust level was quite thin, and I was having trouble with the Time Loss. I stopped research on MPD for a while, I just don't think I was ready to learn more about myself in that area, and started to do research on Biofeedback. I learned that I had Biofeedback while I was in the Service, but I wanted to understand what had gone so terribly wrong.

After doing extensive research, comparing what I could remember to what I read, and came up with the most reasonable theory. I had snapped psychologically and that the Biofeedback just confirmed that. It's what happened after that biofeedback session that was the problem. Let us say that the situation was handled poorly and the outcome was serious in nature.

Back to the MPD, it was apparent that no matter how hard I tried to stuff what I learned about MPD, it kept coming up in my face. There didn't seem to be any escape, except to face the fact that MPD was part of my life, and that I would have to learn how to integrate the information known into my life.

In a class on psychology, I did a research paper on MPD, and I wish to put it in this chapter. I feel that it will give you an idea of what some of the causes are that pertain to MPD. (The numbers are the pages of the Research Paper.)

1

There is much controversy surrounding accurate diagnoses of Multiple Personality Disorder (MPD). Before 1980, approximately 200 cases were reported; this increased to 5000 cases by 1990. MPD is no longer as rare as has been reported, but intervention and treatment are slow going and complex. Studies have shown, that the largest percentage (97%) of people with MPD were victims of severe physical or sexual abuse, the smallest percentage (3%) were victims of neglect, and other forms of deprivation. (Oke & Kanigberg 1991) Accordingly, the methods of treatment for MPD vary from person to person.

This research paper investigates the question "What are the most effective methods of therapy for treating (MPD) using Occupational Therapy? The three major areas of therapy which have been found most effective for treating MPD are as follows:

(1) the assessment process using "The Role Checklist", (2) methods of therapy using Occupational Therapy in a hospital setting, and (3) Principles as a guide for therapists and patients.

It is important to organize the methods of therapy that have been used in treating MPD. A most successful assessment process has been the use of "The Role Checklist". This permits the therapist and patient to view a scale of tests on paper.

2

Alter personalities were able to identify their names, ages, sexes, workplaces, and marital status' clearly. Future treatment areas, particularly the more expressive methods of therapy, were identified by the alter personalities as areas of interest in the checklist. Hypnotism was often used as a tool to gain access to alter personalities, since people with MPD and other dissociative disorders were able to be hypnotized more easily due to their high suggestibility level. Hypnotism has been used to join alter personalities in an integrating process. (The Harvard Mental Health Letter 1992)

The first area of therapy was helping patients to recognize feelings of awareness and practice relaxation techniques to better understand their complex MPD skills. This is done in a safe environment, the therapists, mental health professionals, social workers, and other supporting staff members need to provide clean and caring living conditions.

Patients are taught different coping skills to make them better able to ask for help when needed.

"The Role Checklist," was a great benefit in the case of Amber. By using "The Role Checklist", activity goals were chosen in work, music, and home caretaking.

3

Activities geared in these three areas mentioned were formed with methods of therapy using Occupational Therapy. It is important to emphasize that "The Role Checklist" permitted the alter personalities to meet the therapist directly. The permission of all the involved alter personalities allowed Amber access to all the actual checklists concerning her functioning. These efforts, made on Amber's behalf, gave Amber further understanding, and helped her to obtain more awareness of her other selves, and fostered greater acceptance within herself. (Sepiol & Froehlich 1990)

The second area of therapy pertained to the methods utilizing Occupational Therapy in a hospital setting. Occupational Therapists used several other forms of therapy to prepare the patient for individual or group sessions. These other therapies include; art therapy, movement therapy, vocational counseling, recreational therapy, and horticultural therapy. (Richert & Bergland 1991) In addition, long term psychotherapy and hypnosis are used most commonly. (The Harvard Mental Health Letter 1992)

Commonly used methods of Occupational Therapy include; Playing with toys helps child alters to express feelings non-verbally. Guided imagery is used in stress reduction and to have older alters look after the younger alters.

4

Life skills teaching is used to teach cognitive skills where distortions are common place. Alters are taught constructively and are assured of which feelings are natural; Projective techniques are a form of therapy using paint, drawing, sand play, and clay to express abuses non-verbally. These patients were told in childhood "Not to Tell" by their adult abusers. In addition, Groups are geared for younger alters, so they can communicate with their peers who live in adult bodies, and have experienced similar abuses. (Oke & Kanigberg 1991)

All the methods discussed in this paper have been used through out the world in hospital settings. The treatment services followed a step by step progression from highly structured to least structured as follows:

1. Individual treatment sessions provide specific services for patients who can not cope in group sessions.

2. Unit-based groups were to assist patients in goal attainment and provide encouragement for newly admitted patients. Restrictions within the unit were enforced for patients who need observational

specialized nursing for medical, behavioral, and suicidal risk patients.

3. Centralized groups were for patients attaining levels of responsibility higher than unit-based groups.

5

Patients were given the freedom to come from different units, or patients accompanied by peers or staff members may leave the units. The most trusted patients were allowed to leave their units alone.

4. Leisure skill development groups were to improve social skills in a community setting. (Richert & Bergland 1991)

The third area of therapy covered four principles used as a guide for therapists an patients.

Principle 1: A safe and trusting relationship for the therapist and patient.

Principle 2: Learning becomes more enhanced for patients when it starts at the patient's current functioning level.

Principle 3: Encouragement and validation are key components for furthering the learning process.

Principle 4: Repeated therapy and practice facilitates the patient's learning process. (Angel 1989)

This researcher has investigated the question "What are the most effective methods of therapy for treating (MPD) using Occupational Therapy?" This paper examined the three major areas of therapy most effective in treating MPD.

6

The three major areas explored were (1) the assessment process using "The Role Checklist", (2) methods of therapy using Occupational Therapy in a hospital setting, and (3) Principles as a guide for therapists and patients. The authors cited in this research paper have successfully practiced the methods of therapy for MPD outlined. Given the evidence presented in this research paper, this researcher encourages the therapists, mental health professionals, social workers, and supporting staff members to continue reporting clinical findings and research efforts regarding methods of therapy to patients with MPD. Continued support is essential for new methods of therapy. Occupational Therapy played an important role to recovery in the integration process. It is important to note that this therapy has helped people with MPD not to give up, but to stay functioning in the community setting.

It has been over a decade since this paper was written. There is newer information, but not as much as one would expect. Sexual & Physical Childhood Abuse is still up there in the high numbers despite all efforts in the Department of Children & Families efforts to put a halt to it. But it is no longer these two offenses that is plaguing our country and other countries today. Molestation, Rape, Gang Rape, Childhood Slavery, Adult Slavery, and Ritual Abuses among Occult Groups or Communities, Alcohol and Drugs & Terrorism Extremists are now in the forefront.

Hypnotism is still used for integration, but there are some other methods where the patient with DID (Dissociative Identity Disorder) or MPD (Multiple Personality Disorder) have more active roles in integration of their alter selves.

It's very important that the therapist stay neutral, not take any alters sides or show favoritism. This can totally undermine any good progress already made. I know this to be true by experience. The Alters do need to remember, voice what has happened to them, and then work through the pain to become more healed. I am working at a more spiritual integration with Sam & Tinjcia. I have tried the other ways and they keep coming back. I have to learn to love them and myself. For they are part of me, no one dies. I have learned to embrace them and give them time, but there are rules. Yes, I am married, and it is important that they don't violate those vows. That integration is a win-win-situation, but I don't think they see it that way. It's important that we all compromise and keep a dialogue going.

DID And MPD played a very important role to my and others survival when the abuses were occurring, but now that the abuses have stopped, its important to find our true selves with or without our alters in the forefront. Some of us may have been so damaged that the alter personalities are performing life skills critical to our very survival. That we will just have to stay at our present stage of functioning, because it's the best it will ever be.

If that's the case for me, I will accept my lot, and live out the rest of my days knowing I did my best.

References:

Angel, Susan L. (1989) "Toward Becoming One Self." The Journal of Occupational Therapy. March 7, 1989. 1037-1043.

From Harvard Medical School (1992) "Dissociation and Dissociative Disorders; Part 1&2." The Harvard Mental Health Letter. Vol. 8, No. 9&10, March & April 1992. 1-4ea.

Oke, B. Sc. O.T. (c) Susan: Kanigberg, B.O.T. O.T. (c), Elle. (1991) "Occupational Therapy in the treatment of individuals with Multiple Personality Disorder." Canadian Journal of Occupational Therapy. Vol. 58, No. 5, December 1991. 234-40.

Richert, MS, OTR/1., Gail Z.; Bergland, MFA, MICAT, ATR, Christy. (1991) "Treatment Choices: Rehabilitation Services use by patients with Multiple Personality Disorder." The American Journal of Occupational Therapy. June 1, 1991. 634-38.

Sepiol, MS, OTR/1., Jane M.; Froehlich, MS, OTR/1., Jeanette. (1990) "Use of The Role Checklist with the patient with Multiple Personality Disorder." The American Journal of Occupational Therapy. July 9, 1990. 1008-1012.

More alike than different: Treating Severely Dissociative Trauma Survivors By Margo Rivera

A Fractured Mind: By Robert B. Oxnam

For more information: The Sidran Foundation Web Site WWW.SIDRAN.ORG

I did use "The Role Checklist" for part of my own personal research. The original author of "The Role Checklist" is Francis Oakely , and she lives in Maryland. I thanked Francis Oakely for her help in providing the research material for my own journey and that of my research paper.

I did some of the other tests that Francis had sent me. I was surprised by some of the answers that were written by my alters. Samantha and Tinjcia still aren't fully integrated at this time and may choose to never to do so, I can't worry about that at this time, as long as they behave themselves, I can't complain. I am not about to try and fix something that works for the time being. Forced integrations have a tendency not to last anyhow, so, why push it?

Like any relationship, you have to work with what you have, you can't worry about what you don't have control of, and you focus on only that which is in your immediate grasp.

The rest will take care of itself.

It's better to focus on what you can do than what you can't. If you focus more on what you can't do, you waste a lot of energy, and you can't finish what you can do. With additional research, much of what I have written is still used today. There hasn't been much change in treatment or research since this paper was put together.

5

Vision Techniques:
With Dr. Susan C. Danberg

This area interested my primary doctor, Dr. Bentley was amazed by the information I gave him about the vision problems I was having and how Dr. Danberg helped me understand what I needed to do to correct the problems.

One of the ways was by visual techniques and relaxation. Dr. Danberg was very patient with me as to build trust. Being the professional individual Dr. Danberg is, kind, firm, straight forward, and caring.

During some of these eye examinations, it came clear that other personalities existed. Dr. Danberg approached me with the idea that I was acting different at times and was concerned about my driving. Through using the eye coordination exercises, a few alter personalities revealed themselves and asked for help to be integrated. Dr. Danberg managed to do this successfully. (This doesn't mean the other personalities are dead, they become more whole with the Host Personality. In this case, it is Laura). Only I have found out that no integration really occurred, that the personalities just went away for a while, and that they did reappear a couple years after.

The techniques Dr. Danberg used to treat the eye vision problems are no big deal, but the information the personalities gave for their existence is strictly confidential. Dr. Danberg gave me exercises I had to do to correct some double vision. String with some beads to focus on, some glasses, most of all, and the trust the exercises would be done. It didn't take too much time before things just fell back into place.

The Role Checklist was another method for identifying the alter personalities, the experiences for why I split off into other personalities is too graphic to put down on paper. I made a conscious decision to leave it out. If you have been abused, sexually assaulted or something else that was mentioned in the last chapter, there is no sense in being re-traumatized.

This is a book about life after traumatic experience, and I felt the graphic details were unnecessary. I don't want to traumatize anyone who may be reading this. It holds no healing aspect for this book. (furthermore, everyone's experience is different). In writing this book, it is helping me to heal, and to show others forgiveness and caring by example.

I will not condone the acts of recklessness, neglect, physical or mental abuse of others, but who I am to not forgive others?

We all make mistakes, this is being human, I feel in order to be forgiven for my own wrong deeds, I need to forgive others. That accident changed my life. It also brought to my awareness that their were other parts of myself that needed some serious attention in order for me to live safely in this world.

I would like to take a few moments to say that for me, God had put Dr. Danberg in my life for a certain time to see through the hate and confusion, that one can experience during a traumatic event, you will see that light at the end of the tunnel, and learn to see the journey this life has to offer. (Just a Metaphor).

6

Resolving Conflict (Past & Present)

    This will be a deep chapter into one's soul. Conflict is necessary and how we perceive it, handle it, cope with it, or in some cases we haven't dealt with it, and just a general attitude of how conflict shapes our lives. You may experience a sense that this chapter is very conflictive, bounces around from topic to topic, and/or just hard to grasp. It's not you, it's the chapter. It's suppose to make you feel confused a lot. I geared it that way so that you would get a feeling for how I feel having a traumatic brain injury.
    This chapter has tested my emotions to the further limits of the unknown. The spiritual being of myself and my creator I call God. Not everyone's creator is perceived in the same way, but for myself, God is the reason I still live on this earth.
    The Near-Death I experienced brought me face to face to the Light of this Universe. The God of my understanding, and learning to know what my mission will be. The path to truth can be a bumpy one as I have already experienced. The conflict comes when I realized I was in a different space in time.
    Now I am researching many aspects of what conflict means and how I was affected. The truth really does hurt. To finally face my demons, or my perceptions of what I call demons has brought me

to a stand still. The book I have been reading involving the HOPI Indians has really put me in a state of confusion, and all your getting is my perception of what this book has taught me.

The next sections of this chapter will be right from the heart, a place in which I have been most vulnerable. The Rawest part of myself will be revealed, and not for anyone to criticize or judge. There needs to be a certain amount of respect given to privacy of graphic details I am purposely leaving out because of the trauma that may follow after reading. Anyone who has been serverely traumatized may be able to relate to this warning.

Past Conflict: How Conflict has changed how I viewed myself.

Conflict is essential to problem solving. From the book I have been reading about the HOPI Indian, many conflicts were resolved by councils or tribal input. The conflicts on many aspects were resolved with less hardship and resentments.

I feel the conflicts from my past still affect how I deal with conflicts of today. There has been so much my Dad has taught me on woodworking, learning how to use the tools safely, and just basic survival skills.

We shared a common disease of Alcohol addiction, I was fortunate like my Dad to get help and work a twelve step program that I truly believe saved my life.

Being in recovery has helped educate me, that doing alcohol or drugs isn't going to solve my problems, but probably make them worse. Yet, I was fool enough to think after 17+ years I could go out an drink reasonably. But I have recently learned that it was one of my alter personalities that had the problem. So being on the side of caution, I won't test those waters.

My Dad died on Dec. 6th, 1996. I felt a void, hate, anger, love, compassion, apathy, empathy, and at the end of his life I felt very sad.

Lee cried for a few nights, because I know he missed his Grampa. Dave and I included the children in this death process, and trying to help them to learn that Grampa is in a better place and in no more pain. Gramma Posuniak talked to the Twins and explained the best she could that Grampa was in a better place. It showed a lot of courage on my Mom's part. This really touched my heart to see my Mom show Lee & Keith that they didn't have to fear this death process.

Again, conflict comes in several ways, degrees, shapes, and aspects. How the conflict is dealt with in the here and now is the most important. I feel my soul crying out, reaching for the strength, hope, and compassion. The emotional battle I feel makes my whole body ache. The tears are right there.

The new therapist I am working with says, " This is what Crisis is all about", right in it and I am too numb to even notice or feel it. It's been real hard dealing with Dad's death. I feel tired all the time, I'm not even hungry. Elizabeth Monahan nodded Her head at this and said, "Yes, you knew it would be this hard". Part of my Past Conflict has to deal with an Aunt & Uncle who felt it was their duty to try and turn my brothers and I against our own parents. The Mental & Verbal Abuse from them that has taken along time to resolve. Each person's life is destined to be fulfilled in whatever way the path was chosen, I believe now, that what my Aunt & Uncle did was just them being themselves. As for that Aunt & Uncle, I wish no ill will, and that you have a wonderful life.

To Mrs. M, I pray, that you are no longer abusive, and that you have gotten the help to not be abusive to children as you were to me. May God be with you and your family.

Present Conflict: Dealing with my Dad's death, Panama issues concerning being mugged, focusing on the here and now, being a loving wife and mother, and trying to stay a whole sane individual.

It's time to face the reality of the immediate situations. I have to admit this is a crisis situation, no avoidance will work in this time and space.

It's a One Day at a Time Living Arrangement. "Only doing the basics!".

I know that Dad was very hurt when I joined the ARMY, but that was my decision. I was sick and tired of being told I should just find a man an get married. Mostly said by other classmates and others who just didn't really know me all that well. That a woman's place was at home.

Hearing that statement made me feel like I wanted to punch out the next person who said it. I was too much of a party animal and really wasn't looking for a man in my life at that time anyway.

I wanted to know the truth about the world, that it wasn't always a negative place to live, that if you work hard enough for something you can achieve it, and it's all in the way we look at it. My Aunt telling me I was a coward, was just the straw that broke the camel's back, and there was a lot of issues hitting me at once. That Aunt who called me a coward, has long been forgiven. (But I know it really upset my Mom a lot). I only used that as an example, you can use whatever excuse you would like, but the truth of the matter, it was a career move, and that being a Certified Nurses Aide just wasn't working out well for me. Too many politics before I left. Do the extra's but we aren't going to pay you anymore for doing what isn't in my job description.

Too much abuse even there, I was there to help these old people, and couldn't stand by or cover up for someone's ill temper being taken out on a resident at the Nursing Home I was working for. I was really feeling the stress and feeling burnt out.

There was a lot of discord among some of my co-workers, cutting corners for some jobs, or being a witness to some verbal or physical abuse was getting me into trouble, I just couldn't cover up the abuse, not ever, and that it was hard for me to stay neutral.. There was an R.N. with whom I could always talk to when she was around. Rita or Cynthia or Grace was an Ali I could always trust.

I also went into the ARMY, because I wanted to experience life and fight for my Country. I had a lot of patriotism in me that I knew going into the U.S. ARMY was the place to be. I really wanted to be all I could be.

Even after being Medically Discharged from The Service, when I returned home, I felt like I hadn't been gone. No one wanted to talk about the time I spent in service, because of what occurred down there. The real issue was, they figured I would act like I did before I went into the Service, to their shock, I was different, and I didn't feel respected for trying to Serve my Country, and putting in my time to help keep this Country Free. Although, my Mom respected me more than my Father.

I learned some interesting facts about The HOPI, the different clans, and spiritual rituals.

There were very strict guides and rites that needed to be accomplished before the Natives could be settled down to their right places of habitation. All the clans had to make the cross, meaning, they had to go to all four corners of this Country. Most migrations started from the South, then East, West, and North. If all four migrations weren't accomplished, the clans that didn't finish their migration were usually destroyed, and not always by nature, but by other clans.

Bear, Eagle, Snake, Parrot, and Badger clans were the first to migrate to their settlements.

During the times of migration, several clans would gather to insure safety and get to their settled areas with higher survival rates.

The reason I brought up the issue of the HOPI Indian, was because I feel we have to go through all that we do, to appreciate who we are, what we have made of ourselves, and give back the gift of life God has freely given to us.

With all the conflict I have endured, Dr. Sarah J. Gamble helped me keep some structure to our sessions., Dr. Christopher Bentley helped me stay in touch with health care providers of my choosing, Trish, Rene', Dr. Eva Salzer, Elizabeth Monahan, Paula, Marilyn, Michelle, Susan, and Robin Grant-Hall are helping me with skills & relaxation to keep me in the now.

One of the spiritual ways I learned to stay spiritually and physically grounded was by making peace hangings. My own design to keep me home, busy with twins, but busy to stay at home, and keep me from traveling out of state or country.

Dave has stated that he really needs me, that the twins need me, that although, having lost my wedding band & engagement ring, they are only material things, that we have gone through worse times, and we will get through this also. I had to accept the fact the rings were MIA, and Dave said, "Not to Sweat It!". When I mentioned at the beginning of this chapter, this would be the chapter that goes right to the very soul, I meant that. To share what I have so far would have been considered an act of treason or something like that.

It wasn't hard to leave out details of the early trauma, why re-traumatize myself in the process. It's been a while since I have written anything, but when you're right in the middle of the trauma, one can hardly think, and writing was definitely not one of my functioning motor skills.

I haven't completed the book about the HOPI Indian, but I feel I can finish it soon.

It's about 2:48A.M. Dec.21, 1996, still wide awake, I just can't seem to fall asleep, and this book needed some serious attention.

I had a lot of respect for Dad when he finally decided that his time was finished. It took a lot of courage to do what he did. I believe he was able to make all the amends he could in the extra time he was given.

I do miss him. I know the pain he suffered. Dad knew I knew what would happen. I'll never forget that wink he gave me at the Hospital. Mom hasn't let me forget it, she mentions it all the time. Dad knew I knew the white light was with him all the time, just too damn proud to admit it. I know that he died with Mom in the room and that he wasn't alone.

I didn't understand the hand movements, Dad, I suspected it had something to do with my missing rings. No, I haven't found them.

Dear Dad, I am really confused as to what to write. At least, the program of recovery we chose for ourselves has taught us: Serenity, courage, and possibly wisdom.

In Aunt Jean's Christmas Card to my family and me, my Aunt Jean thanked me for giving her back her brother, I felt happy that I could be of some help, and I really cried real hard, because that whole "Rift Thing" never made no sense at all, actually, it made no dollars either.

In this chapter, you have only gotten one person's experiences in this life's journey, that there has been many before me, and there will be many more when I 'am gone.

This chapter was very heart wrenching to say the least, but it is the truth to the best of my knowledge and ability. I truly believe that I 'am Beating the Odds, with all the love, support, respect, and encouragement I have received.

The hurt has to stop somewhere and what difference does it make who stops it first, as long as it stops, and the healing can begin. Riffs & Secrets are what make people sick is what I believe. And you stay as sick as the secrets you keep.

Make Peace whenever and wherever possible, for one doesn't know when it's their time to go home, and love one another as we are being loved.

7

Learning How to Open Up & Trust

How does one open up & trust when they have been burnt so many times? Trust just doesn't present itself, and opening up often leads to disappointment & resentment. This chapter will challenge my confidence and ability to let others know who the real Laura is, and quite frankly, I have no idea, except that I am a Wife, Mother, Sister, Daughter, and Friend.

I am hoping that by the end of this book, I can be as whole as one could be, and that all the aspects of my life will become one with this body. Life's journey comes with much baggage, but one can choose to leave the baggage behind, and start a new with the God of this Universe that has given us our lives.

Doing a Partial-Trauma Treatment Program at Elm Crest was a start. And, again, Dave my husband brought some serious issues to my attention, and I acted on them accordingly.

I don't know where I would be if it weren't for Dave. This has been a positive approach to a serious problem. I have to say that it can get quite un-nerving at times, but the treatment appears to be working. It's hard to tell from my perceptions. We'll just have to wait and see. I have finished my time at Elm Crest and will be starting a parenting class within a week. I actually got a week off from most of the emotional work.

I feel that this work is to important and I am not willing to let things go by like business as usual. Dave has been my biggest support, safety is No. 1, and I plan on keeping what I have worked for, for so many years. I want the best, I'll have the best, and God doesn't produce junk. It's time for the past negative affirmations to vanish. We live in a new era, and peace is the ultimate goal.

DCF (Department of Children & Family) has been involved, because one of my personalities was becoming violent and abusive, verbally, and physically. Although, I didn't know until Dave told me, that was part of why I landed up at Elm Crest, and among other things. The investigator for DCF told us that she was going to keep the case open until after I completed the parenting class and they saw that things were more stable in the household.

It was hard to have to admit to such events. To stop the damage before it has long lasting effects. It really hurts to know that your kids are afraid of you and don't know why. The therapist I am working with now has made it so that Cynthia, the abusing personality, can't shut me out totally of what she is doing, and that at some level I am still present. Samantha has come back to help me, I welcome her help, and input. Samantha, is another alter personality. There are five besides myself. Laura is the Host Personality: It's time she gets this stuff put in one pot, per say, and then we can enjoy our freedom.

My case has been labeled everything from depression, borderline personality, to a dissociative disorder, and I just can't see why they can't give me the proper diagnoses for what I am experiencing. (MPD- Multiple Personality Disorder). Maybe it's just too complex even for them to understand, yet they don't have to live with me, and I am sure it gets real old.

And just to think, I have just concluded the childhood trauma, wait until I get to the chapter with the Service-related trauma, and I am hopeful that there is a life after all this trauma. Exposing the secrets is one of the most dangerous feats to all this.

A lot of research will be going into this when we get to it. I will close for now. I still have a book I must finish reading. "So, I'll Meet ya all on the Back 40!".

I have three more weeks of the parenting class to go, everything seems to be coming together, and Cynthia gave away her ace card. Meaning that she does plan on leaving, Dave, my husband, is beginning to appeal to her better nature.

I was glad to get that info, I was really beginning to worry if I was going to have to have us committed, to keep her in place with the ground rules we set down for ourselves. She still yells from time to time. The physical and verbal abuse is non-existent. This makes everyone Happy.

It's no picnic havin' DCF involved with ya life, but if we want to keep what we have, ya kinda have to follow the rules they set, and I have been scolded more then a few times for my misbehavior, and I am takin' these parentin' classes very seriously, bein' I am the cause of DCF bein' in their lives in the first place. I hope I can rectify my actions, stay on the straight and narrow, and this is my apology to Laura & Family for what I have caused them in Heartache & Anxiety. Sincerely yours, Cynthia, Alter No.2.

I am happy and in a good place, very peaceful, getting an education, so, I can be a little more grown up. I am six years old, I hope I can come back to finish my integration, I will be doing check-ins to check on progress, and my teacher had to help me put this together.

Love, Southpaw, Alter No. 1.

Stay Tuned in for the next Course of events to occur. I am sure you'll be anything but bored; you might even land up sitting at the edge of your seat for what you are about to read next. Then this may apply to me too. (Finished the Book about the Hopi Indian).

I suggest reading the Book The Hopi Indian by Frank Waters

It really is an eye opener.

My Aunt Helen gave me a few books a few years ago and they are real spiritual.

People of the Earth

People of the Fire

People of the Wolf by W. Michael Gear and Kathleen O'Neal Gear

My Aunt Also gave me the Book For Everything there is a Season An Anthology of the of Father Ralph W. Beiting

It is a shame that the Natives of this New World are still treated with such contempt.

Some may say, "That Bleeding Heart, What do you do with someone like her?"

Please don't judge me, but embrace the knowledge that if it weren't for the Native Americans, none of us would be here this day.

If it weren't for a God of the Universe, would there be life anywhere? Science has proven many Biblical Events, and yet, many of the Scientists don't believe their own findings. What is that all about? More questions than answers I guess.

Spiritualism is a state of mind.

Religion is an institution.

Church is a body of people who share their faith in a Higher Power they call God.

Jesus is the mediator.

F.E.A.R. False Evidence Appearing Real is how Joyce states it in her book Straight Talk Overcoming Emotional Battles with the Power of God's Word.

8

A Loving Tribute to My Mom

Dear Mom,
    This is a Tribute to you for all that you have endured; Love, Substance abuse in the Family, and Dealing with hardship in the Family. I thought real hard before I decided on this chapter, for many reasons, and my heart aches at the thought of having caused such discord. (At least, that is how I perceived it to be).
    This Tribute to you, because of my Love & Respect I have for you. You have endured much and you haven't a clue as how to cope with that. Your Trip to Arizona was quite an ordeal for you to prepare yourself for. Especially since Dad had passed away.
    As that song from "Beaches", The Theme song to "Terms of Endearment", and Kathy Mattea's song "Ready for the Storm" rings out the theme of Love, Survivor, and Warrior comes to mind. You are all of these and more.
    You're the type of Mother any daughter wishes for...
    You were the Peace Maker, you kept the Family Together when everyone wanted to jump Ship, and that takes a lot of courage.
    I wondered how you could deal with what you had, now that I have Family of my own, I know that what you did was out of Love, Devotion, and True Grit.

To focus on the Finer Days is what we have to hold on to. No matter what the past has brought to our future, we have a future, and it's because of you. You showed me the better side of life that I needed to hold on to, and that the recovery program in which I still belong has shown me the Love that is always present.

One Day at a Time, the theme will continue to ring in my ears, the Serenity Prayer Shadow Box you did for me, and to Chill Out.

You have the Strength, courage, and Love that Ruth had in the Bible. I read that on occasion to remind me of my middle name which is my mother's first name. I am honored by that.

You showed me much growing up, what it meant to be a married person, the highs and lows, and the basics for survival as a woman. You have always been No. 1 with me, though, you probably didn't think so, we had a common respect, and I believe we experienced the usual Mother & Daughter confrontations, but I learned from them just the same.

The negative affirmations you have been given yourself in the past aren't true. I don't believe they do anyone any good, and they are hard to hear. We grew up with them, this is the twenty first century and that kind of self talk no longer holds any bearings on this life. It is easier said than done, I know.

That's where Faith comes in, it replaced the Fear I held, and your endurance gave me that Faith. I can only imagine the pain and anguish you suffered. I learned by your example that you can get through anything and that we don't have to do it alone.

This Loving Tribute I give to you Mom, because you are more than deserving of it, you are the Light of your Children's Hearts, and the Strength that you carry is from the One Above. I believe we are all Angels to one another, that our missions in this life are different, that is why we are here, and that Peace is attainable.

Thank you for being yourself, for being my Mom, and for your Love, Support, and Encouragement. This is my Loving Tribute to my Mom, Stay Well, and Keep a Peaceful Heart.

Love,
Ladybug
(nickname since childhood)

9

An Experience with DCF in Our Lives

DCF (The Department of Child and Family). Having them in our lives for six months or better hasn't been a negative experience for me, anyway. I can't speak for my husband, though.

They became part of our lives, because I had slapped one of our sons in the face. To be honest, it had been on more than one occasion, let me state, not knowing what the law is on this, it was upsetting at first. It wasn't until Dave, my husband brought it to my attention that other things were occurring, such as yelling, and being un-manageably disagreeable. It wasn't just with the twins, but with Dave as well.

This all started after another accident. One with a cement truck, "Oh My!", the twins were in the car at the time. This was a horror story gone terribly wrong.

Thank God the twins weren't taken away in the process. We did all we were suggested to do, and more. Judging From the parenting class, this was the rarity, not the norm, and it felt real good to say goodbye to Tracy. Now that the mission was accomplished, a parent aide is coming to the house one day a week to help out, and that is not taken for granted.

It has been really hard to deal with life after being hit by a cement truck. There were so many twists and turns that ya would have needed a road map to find one's own way around here.

Trust was on thin ice. Safety was a concern, and mental stability was running mighty thin.

The anger, hurt feelings, and self-esteem were at their all time worst. It was more like being in a jungle after a battle was fought, sometimes very dark, and other times on the lighter side.

"The STRESS was so THICK, ya could cut it with a knife!". Cynthia is talkin' now. I did git the attitude change that was required, it was very hard to cope with Dave, bein' married was not my idea, but I learned about the perks of bein' married, and the options I was given were fair.

I have more education than what I know what to do with, it has been really rough at times, but when ya mess up, and we all do, then ya got to take the responsibility to clean it up.

I did jist that, I hope that thing's now will be much calmer, and Laura can work on the more important thing's. Such as the twins and Dave. Maybe git some correspondence out that we been puttin' off. I believe there are some individuals who need to hear from us.

P.S. Ya might say we would be havin' our own war here, fightin' for time an all, but I can assure ya, thin's are so much calmer.

Actually, I didn't feel Dave trusted me since the twin and I were hit by that cement truck. Trust just didn't present itself, I didn't really know how bad things had gotten, until after my engagement & wedding band disappeared after Thanksgiving. Today was my last visit from Tracy, our case worker from DCF. I finished my second round of parenting classes, the first was mandated, the second was voluntary. Dave had to go to classes in the evenings, because he worked during the day. We also went for marriage counseling & stress management for a while. It brought us closer together.

Dave was really resentful about the past six months, it was an invasion on his privacy, and yet he got the ball rolling, I just took action.

We received help in several areas, from alternative discipline for children, to getting our children started in a pre-nursery program, because of being twins, and having their own language, it was hard to understand them talk. I heard it would be better to do something early than to wait before they were to old to want to speak.

While I went to parenting classes, daycare was provided in the same building, this helped me better take care of them on days I had class. Participation is important. I learned more about the system of DCF than I had known. That most of the parents didn't have their children living with them, it was hard to hear the parents stories sometimes, being we didn't have the twins taken away, and this wasn't generally the norm.

In conclusion, I have to say that it was a positive experience having DCF in our lives for a while, but there were several pros than cons, and I feel closer to Dave more than when everything hit the fan. We worked it out, it could've ended in divorce like so many other couples, but not every situation is the same, and you can't stay in an abusive household.

Although, many do, and that is tragic. Relationships are a lot of work.

It rained, it poured, been there, done that, and it's over. Not quite, but more to what is comfortable, for me, and I am not sure about Dave, I can't speak for anyone else but myself. Something's have to be worked out by yourself, we can share them with other's, but we have to do our own soul searching, and the journey is whatever you decide to make it.

Having a parent aide come in once a week to help with the twins was a plus. Someone to bounce things off of regarding childcare. Sandra kept structure and taught me how to keep things in perspective.

I had to also learn how to manage my chronic pain from the accident with the cement truck. The pain was so bad sometimes, I just wanted to die. That wasn't an option. But when I finally learned how to manage the pain, life got a lot easier. Not always less painful, but I learned how to ask for help on the bad days, and not overdue on the good days. I am enclosing the Chronic Pain Cycle to Help Others Who may experience chronic pain.

Suggested Reading:

The Chronic Pain Control Workbook A Step-by-Step Guide for Coping With and Overcoming Your Pain By Ellen Mohr Catalano, M.A.

Car Accident: A Practical Recovery Manual- By Jack Smith

Still Me- By Christopher Reeve

The Language of Letting Go- By Melody Beattie

When Angels Speak Inspiration From Touched By An Angel By Martha Williamson, Executive Producer

The Book of Sound Therapy: Heal Yourself with Music and Voice By Olivia Dewhurst-Maddock

10

Memory Recall: (U.S. Army) Tour of Duty

Where do I start this? Today is 30 July 97, it's a Wednesday, and plans for visiting "The Wall" are in place. (The Vietnam Veterans Memorial Wall), all that is connected to the Shrine that has been built for many years, and more to come, I am sure.

Babysitters are all lined up and things ought to go smoothly.

Although, this trip doesn't occur until October and the hubby is gittin' a little nervous. I can say today that it shouldn't be a problem, and yet, this is a sensitive subject for Dave, I believe there might be some resentful thoughts brewing, since Dave's Father rejoined the Military and Dave's Mother divorced him. Everything that happened after that is between Dave and his Father. They do write on occasion and exchange Birthday and Christmas Cards.

I went in the ARMY on a delayed plan, there were things I had to do before I actually left for training. I went to Fort Dix on 12 March 85, the eight weeks I spent there were memorable, sometimes violent in nature, and other times funnier than you can imagine.

Only problem, I lost so much time, I volunteered for everything, my Dad was so depressed by this, and yet, I had something to prove to myself and no one else. I actually enjoyed myself.

I did this for my own growth, I probably did it for all the wrong reasons, but at the time, I felt is was right for me. I didn't have to explain anything to anybody but myself. I drank somewhat heavy, but this was normal for me, and I really didn't feel it was a problem, I either drank or didn't, it didn't matter to me, and that was the truth.

Then there was A.I.T. (Advanced Individual Training), which sent me to Aberdeen Proving Grounds in Maryland. That was an exciting time. Strange though, I don't remember to many events, except, being sexually harassed by a sergeant, almost framed for drugs, and getting kicked on the obstacle course by a C.I.D. (Criminal Investigation Division) individual, who will be left unknown, because I remember very little about her, and to protect her privacy rights.

There was a drill sergeant who kicked me out of her platoon, because I told her, "If you don't take your hand off my shoulder, I am going to lay you out cold!". I guess I really pissed her off by this, and then to top it off, two male drill sergeants fought over who was going to straighten me out, until they heard the reason why I was in trouble, and didn't comment after that. (I guess they felt my answer was justified).

I seemed to unintentionally get myself in more trouble than what was good for me. It just followed me wherever, whenever, and however it pleased. For almost all of the two years I spent in the 193rd Support Battalion, Ft. Clayton, Panama, I became a walking time bomb, and waiting for some individual to set me off. A so-called friend, Munckin got a lot of people in trouble when that journal came up M.I.A.. This was a personal journal, to say the least. The number of people who were taken out of Service because of this journal was astronomical.

There were more Article 15's and court martials than you could shake a stick at. Then there were also the drug cover-ups, frame-ups than you could count on your hands, and toes. Then there was the usual switching of wives and husband's. You would have needed a score card to keep track and that was just the icing on the cake.

I was raped by a fellow comrade, only to be told by MP's that if I pursued the issue and messed up the drug case with a rape charge, I would probably come up missing in action.

That didn't include the threats of harm made to my family back in the states, if I didn't comply with their warnings.

When I was medically discharged from the ARMY, it took me more than ten minutes to decide if I was going home or somewhere else. With the threats, I wasn't sure if I ought to go home, in case something bad happened to my family because of me. That would have been the worse. My attorney from the ARMY said, "I would be safer out of the Service. I knew too much and it would be harder for someone to track me down.

I had to be careful, my older Brother is and Officer in the Navy, and I didn't want anything to happen to him. It was a hard judgment call, but I had to make the ultimate decision, if I stayed in, there was a greater possibility I would be killed. I decided to take my chances on the outside. Although, I would have stayed in if my family safety wasn't threatened. Some would have considered that blackmail. I considered it a betrayal. A few bad apples can ruin a whole bushel. A larger sacrifice I would say.

During this time in Service, I went for some biofeedback, to try cutting down some of the stress and things went really strange. I still get white flashes when I am near a hospital, or being at my appointments at the VA Medical Center. I am too paranoid to get on buses, because I am in fear that there may be a bomb aboard. I was on a bus that got bombed once, and saved 25 others with me.

I am afraid of crowded places. It drives my husband crazy I think, but he hasn't been in situations I have, and I don't expect him to understand, but to just have some patience, and some empathy. I love the Holidays, it's the crowds I have trouble with, and not every time is it a problem. (Just most of the time). There was a bomb scare at the library I was attending for grade advancement. The mention of hospitals leaves me in a vulnerable state of paranoia, because of what happened on one of the psychiatric wards in Panama.

This is the Country Panama, not the city of Panama in Florida.

This is where the fighting before the invasion of '89 took place to catch Noriega. Oliver North was just following orders, the scape-goat you could say, and someone had to be blamed. Why this has to be the case is beyond me, I feel that there were a lot more involved, and if you punish one, you ought to get them all. Or clear them.

I would have liked to have seen the list of Senators or Congress Personnel Noriega had allegedly had?, that was never really cleared up. What happened to that supposed list?, or did it really exist?, and I suppose we'll never know the answer to that?.

I do feel that the Service learned about the MPD (Multiple Personality Disorder), used it to the max, and that is only a theory too. There is no evidence to support such an allegation, but it really makes me wonder how one can forget most of their ARMY Tour of Duty.

Too many if's, what's, shoulda, coulda, woulda's for me to figure out, and one thing I can be sure of, is that I spent a lot of time at that hospital. I did fail to mention I was mugged on two occasions, only one reported, M.I.A. for 48hrs., and drugged on more than two occasions I can think of. This doesn't explain being thrown down a couple flights of stairs, and being on a guard duty that proved to be almost fatal. "Classified" At this point in my life, I guess I really don't need to know. I do still on occasion get these disturbing flashes of things and I don't know the reason behind them. They are disturbing, distractful, intruding, and evasive pieces of memory I can't quite put my finger on.

As I said, "It's probably better that I don't know why, but it does intrude on my personal life from time to time, and they are frightening to say the least!".

I have to say that I have gotten some information on the TBI (Traumatic Brain Injury). I got in the accident of "89. I found out that endorphins don't regenerate themselves. Once they are damaged beyond their use, they are gone. A doctor for whom I will not mention his name to protect his family. Did me wrong, as a professional, he didn't act very professionally, and for this only God can help him now.

This book is about healing, I won't forget what he has done, but forgive, and let justice take its course. I will not make his family suffer disgrace for this mans actions, the family is not who I am having a problem with. I don't wish no ill. I do however, don't condone this man's actions, know that he has passed away, and will not be harming anyone again.

My husband had me watch the Discovery TV Program about this little girl in MN. She had epilepsy so bad, that surgeons removed half of her brain. To my knowledge, this girl is all grown up and hasn't had a seizure since the surgery, and recuperating as well as expected. I figure if this woman can live off half a brain, I ought to be able to live off half my endorphin levels. It is Faith not Fear that has gotten me this far. Its been over 17yrs. since that '89 crash, I am still breathing, walking, and a few other things.

Doctors don't have all the answers, mine keeps wondering how I do it, and I keep telling him, "Its my Higher Power whom I call God!".

ITS PART OF THIS LIFE CIRCLE AND THAT YOU CAN BE A VICTIM WITHOUT PLAYING THE VICTIM ROLE.

OUR TOUR OR DUTY IS CHANGED FROM GUARDIN' OUR COUNTRY TO GUARDIN' OUR HOME FRONT. LAURA STILL NEEDS HELP WITH HER ATTITUDE AND ANGER LEVELS. THESE PROBLEMS DIDN'T HAPPEN OVER NIGHT AND WON'T GO AWAY IN THE SAME MANNER.

IN A WAY, I FEEL MORE INTEGRATED. DID I SAY THAT? I GUESS ITS TRUE.

THAT MY SERVICE TIME, WHETHER IT BE IN THE SERVICE TO MY COUNTRY OR BEIN' A CIVILIAN, THE DRESS CODE HAD TO CHANGE. WITH THE COMPLIMENTS WE HAVE BEEN RECEIVIN' HAVE BEEN MOST FAVORABLE. I FEEL MUCH MORE CONFIDENT TO LET GO & LET GOD. I AM SURE THERE ARE STILL TROUBLE SPOTS, BUT I NO LONGER FEEL THE NEED TO PICK UP ARMS, AND GO OFF FIGHTIN' WHERE I HAVE NO RIGHT TO BE.

IN ANY CASE, NOW I HAVE A FAMILY TO WATCH OUT FOR, WHO CARES WHAT NAME IS USED, PEOPLE ONLY SEE AND KNOW LAURA ANYWAY.

THIS BRIN'S TEARS TO MY EYES, TO MOURN THE LOSSES OF THE PAST TO THE LIGHT. I RECKON MY ENCOUNTER WITH ONE OF THE BROTHERS I WAS IN COMPANY WITH IN A FEW SHOOTIN'S ATTACKS IN THE DOWNTOWN REGIONS OF PANAMA WAS VALIDATIN' ENOUGH FOR ME. I KNOW I SHOULD HAVE USED A LITTLE MORE RESTRAINT FOR LAURA'S SAKE, BUT THAT HAS BEEN ONE OF MY BIGGEST PROBLEMS. ITS NO WONDER LAURA WAS GETTIN' OVERWHELMED.

MORE LIKE OVERWHELMED PERIOD. HAVIN' ONES PAST COME OUT IN FULL GRAPHICS, IS JUST TOO MUCH. LAURA HANDLED HERSELF WELL CONSIDERIN' THE TOPIC AT HAND. D.H. IS STILL AMONGST THE LIVING POPULATION. AT LEAST, I KNOW I DIDN'T IMAGINE MY RELATIONSHIP WITH HIS BROTHER. THOSE WERE WILD DAYS.

I SUPPOSE STAYIN' IN THE PRESENT IS MORE IMPORTANT THESE DAYS, THAT GOIN' OFF IN PAST ATTITUDES NO LONGER WORKS, AND THAT'S NOT SURPRISIN'.

I RECKON THIS IS FOR THE BEST IN THE LONG RUN, AS ROBIN PUT IT, "WE HAVE TO PUT SOME OF THESE ACCIDENT ANNIVERSARIES TO REST!". I SUPPOSE ITS OKAY TO LOOK, BUT DON'T STARE, AS JOE R. PUTS IT. I GUESS I HAVE BEEN STARIN' TOO LONG.

TRAILIN' OFF FOR NOW,

SAMANTHA

Just to jog your memory, I mentioned in a previous chapter about not feeling grounded, and that I felt I no longer belonged down here. The doctor said, "It was impossible that half my endorphin levels were not working!". This doctor was the top in his field of expertise, he didn't even want to believe in his own findings, and what's that all about other things that happened after were unprofessional and unethical.

It's taken over 17yrs. for the truth to finally come out. May be I can get some closure to that whole accident issue surrounding the '89 crash, that put my whole world as I knew it into a constant state of upheaval, and get on with my life. ("Easier said than done!").

Granted, I have been a functioning individual, but on what level? I want to do better by my family and myself. I wanted to share these experiences that may be whoever reads this might do something different and not go through the horrors in the medical profession that I had to experience.

I want to help educate doctors and other professionals in the medical field to be more open to the possibilities of TBI suffers. The family suffers just as much as the person with the injury, sometimes worse, because they feel helpless in their inability to help the person with the injury. That's my own personal experience.

I truly believe that Europe is far more advanced in medicine than we are, in the Native American and Central American Shaman's culture there's also more advancement. But it can go both ways.

I do not regret my somewhat colorful past, it has been sometimes extremely dangerous, and destructive in nature. I don't think I would ever go back to change what has happened, but I doubt very seriously that I would wish it on my worse enemy either, and that is no lie. I will write about my experience of going to "The Wall". The two years, four months I spent in the ARMY are memorable to a point, and incredible on other points.

17 October 97, what a day. The Amtrak Train Trip to Washington D.C. was a bumpy ride. With all the excitement of preparing for this trip, I didn't get much rest prior, but I did sleep like a rock on this night, and so did my Sister in Arms. I don't think I would have done it alone. I am sure Dave wouldn't have considered taking me, but I hadn't asked him to. I didn't have a whole lot of expectations about how I was going to cope with all the triggers this trip would bring up.

I was so far in left field, I didn't know what all the hype was about this weekend we had planned to go, it finally sunk in at the Dedication of the New Commemorative Stamp made for all the Women Vets who Served, although, if it weren't for the Men's support, respect, and thanks, it might not have meant as much.

I did feel so much more validated by this Dedication Ceremony, and the Evening Events just put me in a state of awe. The whole day just moved in slow motion for me, it was fun marching, and singing cadence with all the Women from all over the World. The Film Clips from the News Stations and News Papers really didn't catch the air of Mutual Love, Care, and Respect that we were all there together to share.

There was the usual Political Hype there has always been. Yet, this a time dedicated to the Women who Served, and if one wishes to get technical, we all needed each other.

Whether it is Peace Time or a time of War, both genders were thrown in the mix together, and having a Male Veteran come up to me and Thank me for Serving brought me to tears. The Veteran gave me a hug. I was so moved by this.

Washington keeps wanting to segregate us Women from the Men, but when it comes to War, both genders suffered torture, all good soldiers know what they are signing up for when they sign on that dotted line, and say their Service Pledge to their Country.

The War hasn't necessarily ended for those who were wounded, in whatever way, physically, mentally, or emotionally. Many are still homeless from the Vietnam War, or in jail, or if you were courageous enough to get help, and get your life back is a miracle. Many Veterans, including myself, may have gotten involved with mission work, had a faith they could use to help other Veterans. Sometimes to just sit and listen to a Veteran tell his or her story is enough to brighten their day.

Trauma is still trauma, drugs are drugs, and a Rose is still just a Rose. We are who we are, some of us just have more baggage than others. Communication is what breaks the barriers. Breaking the assumption habit and lower expectations is part of what makes the healing process a little easier to cope with.

I could probably write a book just on this Iraq War itself, but not right now, too political for me, and I am sure there would be death threats, so why put myself, and my family through that.

But I will admit, I would have picked up arms if ordered to by my Country, and I am not ashamed of that. Our U.S. Service Men & Women need all the support they can get, here at home and overseas. Many other Countries would probably like to see the U.S. be divided and conquered, this is why we all need to stay United, and determined. My feelings of the Middle East are split. I know they're a lot of good people who need help in the Middle East, but who are we to throw our weight around?, and change their whole culture? Unless it's something they really want?

I have read the Koran twice, their prophet was assassinated, ours was crucified, and to love one another instead of killing one another is the better way to go. Unlike what is happening now. We are all God's Children to every breath we take in. Calling each other names isn't going to solve the problem nor is killing each other with bombs.

I give these sorry individuals credit for one thing, they are willing to die for their cause, and that is tragic. Some are teenagers that were brainwashed and misguided. What's with our own teenagers who are killing other students and teachers, because they were bullied? May be they don't feel they get enough attention. I don't feel these kids who kill others in their schools deserve any publicity from News Stations. Only to say, "They Couldn't find another avenue to take out their aggressions, but to kill others, how tragic!".

I had my share of being bullied and I stood up to them. Some were even better ignored, why be jailed or killed because someone thinks they are better than me. They have their opinion. I don't have to agree with it, but I don't have to hurt or kill anyone for it either.

May be when people finally get the picture that we aren't living according to "The Big Picture!", may be they will realize we all make up a Democratic Society gone mad, that We The People are responsible for the chaos in which we all live today. There is a saying, "EVIL THRIVES", when good people do nothing! By Della Reese, "Touched by An Angel".

Many stories on TV express that very thought, as Touched by an Angel, The Promised Land, even the show Kung Fu, The Legend Continued, and Early Edition.

As you can see, We all are living in the War Zone. It isn't just left to the jungles of some far away country, but is in our own back yards. When are we going to take back our lives, and be accountable for our actions?

By the time we reach Heaven, it will already be too late. That is a fact we will all have to face and that is no lie.

If anything, my visit to Washington D.C. showed me how far away from my true self and who I really am. It's time for me to get real with myself, not blame others for things I haven't wanted to do myself. It showed me the hard facts of what I need to do for myself to be more of who I am and not who or what others think I ought to be.

Dave, my husband, has been real good at keeping things in the now. We all have our handicaps, and learn to compensate for that. We all have Strengths & Weaknesses.

There is more to what we see, seeing isn't necessarily believing, and words are often misinterpreted even to the keenest listener. It's the assumptions that always get us into trouble, because of events taken for granted.

Freedom does come with the Highest Price Imagined. No money is acceptable, it's paid by how we all live. No life or death is truly a waste, only to those who can't think beyond their own lives say, "Young peoples' or infants' deaths are a waste!".

No Ones' death is ever a waste, it can't be compared to life, no matter what age you are taken Home. Sometimes the reasons just aren't clear to us, and only God of our understanding has to really know.

I still feel like I am living on a Tour of Duty. I am a Daughter, Sister, Friend, Wife, and Mother. I feel like my Tour of Duty being a Wife & Mother is more than Domestic by any means, that history needs to be told as it really occurred, and traumatic experience has formed many of our lives.

"We are exactly where we are meant to be in the Here & Now!". Only Fools can fool themselves into thinking otherwise.

WELL I RECKON THAT IT'S ABOUT THAT TIME TO BRING OUT THE TRUTH OF OUR TOUR OF DUTY IN THE U.S. ARMY. IN PANAMA.

SAMANTHA HERE, IT HAS BEEN OVER A YEAR SINCE OUR TRIP TO D.C. IT WAS VERY MEMORABLE, IT TOUCHED THE DEEPEST PART OF OUR SOULS, AND

LEFT US SO MUCH MORE VALIDATED FOR THE TIME THAT WE SERVED.

LEAVIN' TO GO HOME WAS A TUG ON OUR HEART STRINGS, WE WEREN'T GLAD WE WERE COMING HOME, THAT IT WAS A REMINDER OF FEELING LIKE WE FAILED TO COMPLETE OUR MISSION, AND

MAKING THE SERVICE A CAREER. IT WAS A CLEAR REMINDER THAT WE DON'T ALWAYS GET WHAT WE WANT.

IT SEEMS THAT THERE IS NO COINCIDENCES WHEN IT COMES TO TRAUMA. KINDA HARD TO ADMIT, BUT HERE IT IS, AND I HAVE TO GO ON TOO. IT WILL BE NICE NOT HAVIN' TO PROTECT LAURA. SHE IS DOIN' GOOD FOR HERSELF, AND IS MAKIN' BETTER CHOICES. "NOT!".

I RECKON THAT LAURA FELT IT WOULD BE BEST IF I FINISHED THIS CHAPTER. SHE STILL DOESN'T HAVE A LOT OF MEMORY TO ALL HER SERVICE CAREER. MANY OF THE MEMORIES HAD BEEN BLOCKED FROM HER. THAT SHE HADN'T LIED ABOUT HER PAST CHILDHOOD ABUSES. IT DIDN'T EVEN COME TO AWARENESS UNTIL AFTER THE TRAUMATIC BRAIN INJURY OCCURRED IN '89. LAURA CAN NOW START SHARIN' MORE ABOUT HERSELF TO DAVE. KNOWIN' THAT SHE REALLY ISN'T CRAZY, THAT OTHERS WERE WITH HER AT THE TIMES SHE WAS SHOT AT. THAT THIS STUFF REALLY DID HAPPEN.

VERIFIED MANY YEARS LATER.

I KNOW LAURA HAS TROUBLE WITH THIS. SHE IS GOIN' TO HAVE TO TRUST HER HEART ON THIS ONE. BEIN' THAT DAVE HAS ALWAYS BEEN IN HER CORNER IS ALL THE MOTIVATION SHE IS GOIN' TO NEED. ONLY SOMETIMES, HE CAN BE A PROBLEM, AND THIS IS ONE OF THE REASONS I HAVEN'T LEFT YET.

I RECKON ALL THAT HAS BEEN NEEDED TO SAY IS SAID. AS SPOCK ON STAR TREK WOULD SAY, "LIVE LONG AND PROSPER!".

IT'S BEEN A REAL ADVENTURE. MAY BE THIS WILL HELP GIVE YOU THE CONFIDENCE, STRENGTH, COURAGE, AND ENDURANCE TO CONTINUE THIS JOURNEY YOU HAVE EMBARKED UPON. AFFECTIONATELY, SAMANTHA

It is 5yrs. Since my trip to Washington D.C. This book still isn't finished.

Laura here. There has been so much happening since our trip 5yrs. ago. I feel there are some areas that need to be updated.

Memories still coming out in a trickle. There's no rush, it's not like I am going anywhere. I still get the white flashes, buses still bother me, can't stand close quarters, and crowds are still a problem. Just something I'll have to deal with as the problems arise.

Many of the issues written in this book still apply today, I am really working on getting through the issues, but not all the information is reliable, and I haven't got all the information to state all the claims, because of the time out of Service, and my lack of communication with past comrades. Which at this point is not existent.

Privacy? or just Protection? Or both?

I put myself too far into isolation in the last 15yrs. that I lost many of my contacts. No one else's fault but my own. Life just got too busy for me, I got stressed out, and then I went into anger mode.

I'll be going back to anger management once the kids go back to school, it was too hard to expect them to behave for 90 minutes, and I had other things that kept me busy. I needed the individual sessions to work on my sanity, I thought that was more important, and I soon learned that I wouldn't be needing anymore anger management.

The TBI has a factor in this. What classes I do have is enough to keep things at a dull roar. The doctor told me I could continue, but it wouldn't change the damage that has effected the part of the brain that controls impulse with anger. I took the doctors advice, because the evidence was already confirmed.

Through the VA Medical Center, I get crafts to do, and it keeps me out of trouble. I have written a couple of Poems that have gone

National and have won Second Place in the National Standing for the VA Creative Arts Contest. I would like to add them in this chapter. I would like to add one that received a blue ribbon. I have to say, "I am feeling very blessed by the people God has put in my life!", and there is much gratitude for those who have supported me all these years since I have gotten out of the Service.

First Second Place National Winning Poem: 2004

HEALING A SHATTERED SPIRIT

What does that mean? Healing a Shattered Spirit

One has to become spiritual with the self and gain only what Nature supplies.

It was a gray and busy day

I drove to the West Haven VA

It was an exciting ceremony for me getting a National Veterans Creative Arts

Competition Certificate for participation

The Entertainment for this ceremony was grand

My excitement was so grand that I could hardly stand

My heart pounded and my ears rang, because it was so grand

As I left the West Haven VA that fateful day

I witnessed a terrible accident on my way home that day

And life changed that day

The man who caused that accident that fateful day

Passed away in such a frightful way I have to say

The scene could print a thousand words one might say

Four other lives were affected that day

I was lucky that my vehicle wasn't damaged

Yet, within a weeks time the aftermath started to

Creep through my body in a very strange way

First came the anger and the rage

Then there was guilt and shock

How about adding some sadness and unbelief

And then there was depression to boil in a pot

Let it sink in for a week and this is what we got

Life not worth living as our lot

I went through 4 to 5 weeks of intensive day treatment

The days were full of classes for this and for that

I learned how to breathe

And not to seethe

To sit with my feelings

In all of my dealings

When it comes down to healing

This spirit has experienced a lot

I hope with this poem I can express how I felt on

That fateful November day

When my spirit crashed and the journey it has

Taken to put me on the right way

And I am coming full circle to who I am today

The Blue Ribbon Award winning poem: 2005

A WOMAN VETERAN: SHATTERED SPIRITS

The visions I see haunt me. Why do they come to me? Are the visions answers? Or truth? Have I become aloof? Or some kind of spiritual sleuth? Where does the spirit go? I know. I've been there more times than you know.
It's April 18th, 2004, on to Gettysburg is where we go. As a child, there was a threat of war, but now we are at war, it's near and far, with many scars. The first time I visited Gettysburg, it was over 30 years ago. The time was just as wild when I was just a little child.
As I walked around Gettysburg with my family by my side, time slips by with the tide, with my eyes open wide. I have seen much death, not just combat or car accidents. So many wounded, I losing life, and limb.
The day after, we went back to Gettysburg for a longer look, we got caught up in child's play, shooting pop guns, and playing dead. I felt the presence of the dead, my thoughts swarming in my head.

A gift, I suspect, no something I can neglect, what a selection that has my attention.
My life changed since my military tour, many women are so rearranged with the changes in the Corp. Arlington was another venture that tore at my heart and it gave me such a start. There was a funeral that day, with a horse driven carriage on its way, when the sky was turning gray, on that spring day.
I walked through the Women's Memorial with my family by my side, there was so much pride, with my family by my side, and it was important to me. There was so much to see and I am glad they could see the changes in me.
Time passes all to strong, I feel time as it slips by, and all I want to do is cry.

And now my second, second Place National Winning Poem: 2006

The Pains of War

The water at the sea shore doesn't carry the pain out to sea. The pain stays embedded in your soul like sand on the sea floor. With help, you can learn to release the demons from your soul. It takes time to release the pains of war on this turbulent shore.
With years of faith I have overcome many things, yet, it is I who still stumbles in the dark, and pains of war scarred my soul so deep, that it is so hard to sleep.
As I marched in the 2005 Veterans Parade, I had to keep reminding myself where I was. I could feel my heart pounding in my ears, my heart raced in my chest at such a fast pace, yet, no tears ran down my face. How can I keep up this pace? Even with the evidence in my face, I feel like a real space case.
As our convoy traveled forward to the front, the bullets wheezed by our heads, we lost a gas truck, three good guys, and all we could say, "Damn Fools got themselves killed!".
You can't stop the mission, you don't have time to think, you have to keep moving, we'll have time to grieve for them later, but for some reason, grieving never comes, and you either drink or drug it away.

The pain sets up house keeping of it's own. You get so far away from who you really are, that you're not only unrecognizable to others, but to yourself. You feel lost and trapped.
This doesn't get washed away by the sea, it's too embedded in your soul. The waves are strong but your will to hang on is even stronger. You feel your tour of duty is who you are, if someone were to strip away that last piece of your identity, you will vanish, lost forever, trapped in the abyss of pain that has become your whole life. Or what you have perceived it to be.
This goes on for many years and decades, you are feeling depressed, sad, or angry. It creeps up on you while you sleep, or may be while you are still wide awake, and faces of those you have killed come to you in your dreams or waking hours in flashbacks, hallucinations, or delusions.

The Memories are tragic, the lives affected are forever entrenched in our heads, the pain has forever scared the veteran, their families, and friends. The pains of war don't get washed away on the sea shore. You have to learn how to let them go.

Suggested Readings from this Chapter:

The Wolfhounds-By Reverend Joseph David Smith

The Unknown Soldier-By Michael Hastings

Pearl Harbor-By Randall Wallace

God Bless America: Prayer & Reflections for Our Country-By Zondervan Gifts

From Now On…-By Ralph Shallis

11

Near-death Experiences and Common Side Effects

Near Death Experiences are generally caused by traumatic events, whatever they may be: accidents, a head injury, drug overdose, cardiac arrest, and other numerous possibilities.

Although, it is known that NDEs can be caused by euphoric episodes, medication, and other spiritual experiences.

Only problem with any experience, there is the aftermath, and how the experiencer is expressing their particular experience. Many experiencer's have been left feeling invalidated, that what they experienced was some type of oxygen deprivation, and other pneomineons to the like.

I felt really crazy and out of control, it was hard to express what was happening to me, and I kept it to myself. The times I did try to talk about it, it just made me sound really crazy, although, this is only my own perception, it was really driving me insane, and help did eventually get my way. It's literally taken me years to become comfortable in my own skin.

I was referred to the Friends of IANDS, which stands for International Association of Near-Death Studies, that was an avenue that really changed my life, and that of my boyfriend. (In which, became my Husband a few years later). Dave didn't know me before the accident in '89, everything He learned was what I was learning for a second time around, and this was often frustrating, and unstable.

He would call them past lives, the fact that I knew I would marry Dave, and have twins was part of the Tunnel Experience in which I had experienced. I knew a lot about Dave, He wondered how I got the information, background checks weren't necessary, because I had already gotten the approval of the Highest Power known to man, and that there was something about Dave that reassured my knowledge of him.

Through a fellow classmate in High School used to go out with him, she would always talk about how incredibly sensitive he was, that this was something she really liked in him, she hadn't ever given me a last name, but when Graduation came and went, she moved to California, away from the man she said, "She really loved!".

Her loss, my gain, and no regrets. The NDE for me changed me from being a "Material Girl", that possessions no longer held any value to me, I worked on my Family Tree before the accident of '89, went to Poland for three weeks in the Spring of '88, and became even more grateful for the Journey I was embarking upon, which at the time before going to Poland, I stopped drinking, and I knew there was more to life than how I was presently living.

As I wrote in Tunnel Knowledge, I learned about what my life was going to be, although, with a TBI, (Traumatic Brain Injury), Doctors weren't too hopeful of my life expectancy, I was given about 2yrs. left to live, it was definitely a death sentence to say the least, and I am happy to report that I have lived many times past that expectancy, and still evolving to share my experience with others. (And which, I feel like I am back on the same life level as everybody else in the world).

Writing this book has been a healing tool, it has showed me that I no longer have to worry about a physical death, that my journey is in spreading the message that everything matters, and not to take ones good health for granted.

This is not a luxury I can afford, I have to live one minute, hour, day, week, month, or year as it comes, and that goes the same for everybody in the world. I have had to educate myself, and others about what happens to experiencer's. That means any type of Traumatic Experience.

There is a Life After Traumatic Experience, that there is a process which we will all go through at some point or another, there ought not be a label or stigma attach to it. As an experiencer of many things, I am far from being an expert, that mastering myself has been a life battle, and turning it more into a Mystery to be Experienced, and not a Problem to be Solved.

Those who have not taken the risks to experience a lot of different things have taken this for granted in others, that those who have had NDEs, not all NDEs are positive to those who have experienced them, and it wasn't until my third NDE that I learned about the two prior to that.

They're a lot of variables that are distinct to each person, each experience, and no two will ever be alike. There will be similar events, but other variables, and mine is the only experience I can really speak about.

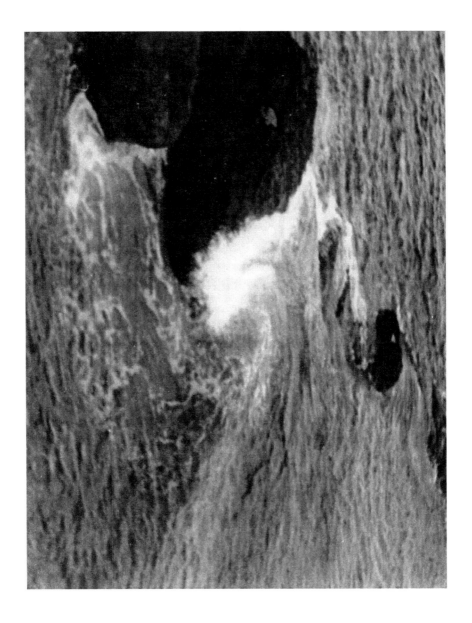

I guess that saying, "When Things get Tough, the Tough get Going!", is exact. At least for me, but there is a down side to that, and everyone suffers. Families can really be uprooted, everything that was taught earlier in life has a different perspective, and learning how to share your experience with family is difficult. (Difficult is an understatement in this particular case), Just when I thought things couldn't get worse, was I mistaken, and what I learned about myself was very discouraging.

How is the family affected? In everyway the experiencer is, and I feel maybe a little more in the sense that they didn't have the experience themselves.

Several variables include, isolation, rejection, alienation, wishful thinking, questioning every decision, control issues, parenting issues, physical relations change, fearlessness sometimes, dissociative behavior, trustworthiness is questionable, over-reactions, under-reactions, loss of roundedness, time boundaries exceeded, personal boundaries invaded or unknown, personal self-esteem, and confidence shattered. I am sure this list can be endless, but I will stop with what I have mentioned. You have to say, "NO, I've had enough!".

How did I get out of the vicious cycle of pain? The pain was physical, emotional, and spiritual. It took a lot of patience, trust, rebuilding of healthy boundaries, relaxation, and therapy in all areas to regain a sense of self I could cope with, address the new physical challenges I have to face in the walking area, the spiritual wall that has been isolating me from the church of my understanding, dropping unreasonable expectations, and relying more on faith & time to heal me.

Plus the physical exercise, taking care of the twins, and keeping a house looking presentable. Knowing that sometimes I will have to ask for more help, and letting the person I ask to do the job, to do it.

I am not doing this alone, that we are all affected in some way, shape, and form.

This also makes everything more manageable, less solitary, and more fun. Can't forget Fun. Making the things that are important fun, using more language, setting an example for the Twins to speak more English, instead of the twin language they like to revert back to on occasion, being consistent, structured, and yet, flexible.

Just be yourself, do what you feel you need to do, and follow through. All you can do is your best. That has to be enough.

12

Going to the Light After the Twins Were Born

The whole pregnancy was difficult. After Lee & Keith were born, and the doctor started to massage my abdomen, I just about jumped off the delivery table. The pain was real horrific, the Nurses' sent Dave out of the room. I don't think I was doing too great, and all I could see was this warm peaceful light on me.

I realized at that moment where I was. I had been at this light before, I didn't go through any tunnel this time. No one ushered me out of this light, and I was a bit confused.

I guess the decision was left up to me this time, there was no doubt where I had to be. I had just given birth to a set of twins. There was no way I could go anywhere else, but back with Dave, and the twins. I am sure I could have gone to Heaven, but then I wouldn't be there to raise the twins, and be with my loving, supportive husband.

Dave says, "He hasn't done much of anything", but he is so wrong, and that without him I wouldn't be as happy as I am now.

I came back to my body. This turned out to be the fourth NDE I have had. I am not having any other children. My husband didn't want me to have a tuballigation, so he got fixed so we wouldn't have any more children. The twins were a miracle birth.

I was told growing up, that I wouldn't be able to carry any children, because of the B- blood w/the RH Factor, and didn't expect to. I had one or two miscarriages in the ARMY. One definitely, the second is questionable, but one recorded pregnancy for sure.

I learned a lot from that fourth NDE though. It definitely set my priorities, gave me love far from what I had known before, and the insight of how to love back. This is not an easy task. I feel fortunate that I had all that guard duty in the Army, four hours on, and four hours off. Although, with the twins' feeding time, it was three hours off, and one hour or so on.

It was still a challenge just the same. I was a night person, as a general rule, but to become a day person. Well let me say, "It took a longer time for me to adjust to days", and that is no lie.

The twins' set their own time of waking up, usually after Dave would leave for work. It was still quite an adjustment. It has been successful just the same.

13

Another Story of a Near-death Experience "A Second Chance", By Mrs. Jennifer L. Babb Davis

Disclaimer: The views or opinions may or may not be shared by the Writer or Publishers of this book, it is another story of an NDE, and the choices this individual took in their personal experience. It is often the Norm, that NDE Experiencers have a high divorce rate, ratio of 7 out of 10 marriages that fail due to the Traumatic changes in the NDE Experiencers life and Family.

"A Second Chance", By Mrs. Jennifer L. Babb Davis

In January 1985, I had an experience that changed my life forever. My husband and I were living in Yokohama, Japan with sons, Teddy, 2yrs, 4months, and Tony, only 4 months old at the time.

I had several miscarriages previously and this had been a very difficult pregnancy. I needed gallbladder surgery, but decided by the fifth month to put it off until after giving birth, I didn't want to lose the baby or put him at risk unless it was a life or death situation for me. The baby was born on September 28, 1984, two years and a day after the birth of his older brother, Teddy.

After 36 grueling hours of drug-free labor, my husband delivered a healthy son. I was so thankful that our baby was okay and I put all my energy into our two little boys. Since I was breast feeding, I decided to put off the surgery for as long as possible, but by mid-January of '85, and I was in so much pain that I knew the surgery had to be scheduled right away. Ted, my husband, was in the U.S. Navy, and stationed in Yokosuka, Japan at the time. I met with a Navy Surgeon at the Military Hospital to discuss having my tubes tied at the same time. I didn't want to be away from our baby and toddler any longer than necessary.

Combining the two procedures seemed like a great idea. I'd be hospitalized for only 3 to 5 days and have an 8 week recovery period at home. I had so much to live for, it never occurred to me that my life could end or be dramatically altered in the blink of an eye.

But, it was, and nothing could have prepared me for that.

I was mentally prepared for the double operation to be performed, by two skilled Naval Surgeons whom I felt confident and comfortable with, I said a little prayer before going under general anesthesia, and wasn't afraid. I'd be home within five days and would feel better as each day passed.

The operations went well, although, I had an upper abdominal incision about 6" long, a lower incision 3" long, and I was anxious to get out of bed and speed up my recovery through movement. I'd just turned 24 yrs. old and wasn't one to lay back and be waited on.

For the first 24 hrs., I was in a lot of pain, but was up, walking about, and doing quite well. The next day however, I noticed a different pain that got increasingly worse, as I rested motionlessly, and for two hrs. my chest tightened until I could hardly breathe.

I finally called the Nurse, immediately, a medic was in my room listening to my chest, He was alarmed by what he heard, and firmly told me not to move at all. Doctors filled the room, I felt helpless, chest x-rays, an angiogram determined the problem, and it turned out to be a Pulmonary Emboli. I found out that this meant I had several blood clots in each lung.

I was taken to ICU, put on oxygen, blood thinners in hopes of preventing more clotting activity, and I was in bad shape. I couldn't get enough air in my lungs on my own, to speak was near to impossible, still not grasping the severity of my situation, and doctors stressed the importance of breathing deeply, relaxing, and thinking positive. I wanted my husband to stay at home, take care of our children, while we waited for me to get better. All I could think of or be concerned for, was our babies.

I was alone in ICU, since the woman who had been in the next room died from a single blood clot in one lung. I finally realized that this could happen to me as well, I started paying close attention to any changes I felt within. My pain began to increase at the wounds, which were heavily bandaged, and taped. I rang for a Nurse to check them, A young Corpsman came in, but never looked at the incisions, He just gave me a shot for the pain, still the pain was increasingly getting worse, and I was really getting worry.

I felt the bandages, the areas felt larger, I couldn't sit up or move, much so, I wasn't sure what was happening to me by that point. I realized I must be bleeding internally, Less than 24hrs. after being put on blood thinners (Coumadin & Heprin), my bleeding increased at the two incision sights.

Time was passing by, I called for help again, only to get another shot of pain killers, and they didn't seem to have much affect. I called again, but this time I asked if the bandages could be loosened, that they were too tight, the corpsman said, "He could do that much!", and when He saw what was happening, He ran out of the room, not to be seen again, and I began to cry. Suddenly, I knew without a doubt, that I was bleeding to death, and from that moment, I prayed non-stop.

Nobody was there to help me, I was frantic, just then, like an angel sent from Heaven, the Navy Chaplain entered my room, She had said a blessing for my youngest son before we brought Him home from the Hospital, and now I felt close to Her. We had a special connection, I immediately pulled up my hospital gown and cried, "They're letting me bleed to death!", She looked at the upper wound, which was the size of a football, and the lower one was that of a grapefruit. The blood was beginning to leak from the bandages by now.

The Chaplain called for a doctor, phoned my husband, who was already on His way to visit me, I was out of my head with pain, I just wanted to kiss my babies one last time, and say goodbye to my husband.

I figured I wouldn't be doing that ever again, the Chaplain had returned to my side, and we prayed together. She was at the head of my bed, praying in my ear. I was crying.

Finally, approximately, four hours from the time I first felt something wasn't right, rang for the Nurse, and my Surgeon rushed into the room. Medical people were all around my bed, by this time, I could barely see or hear anyone, the Surgeon got real close to my face, loudly saying, "Jennifer, I must relieve the pressure right now, there's no time to numb the area!". The Chaplain was still holding my left hand and praying.

I could feel my head moving from side to side, my eyes were open wide, but everything was going black, I knew it was the end, Still I said, "Just do it, cut me, I am dying!".

The Surgeon took the scalpel, slashed both wounds, and I immediately felt relief, The last thing I said was, "It feels like hot syrup is pouring all over me!". Then I was gone.

From the upper right hand corner of the room, I looked down on this poor woman, Her torso was covered with fresh blood, and rolled towels were being press into the newly re-cut wounds on Her body.

Medical people were running in and out of the room.

The woman was being hooked up to IVs and large machines. There was no pain whatsoever. The woman was free. From the top of the room, I couldn't help feeling sorry for Her, so much was happening to Her body, and She wasn't even there. It was just a shell in the bed. The scene was so intensely sad, I couldn't watch, and I had to look away. I looked up and noticed there was no ceiling in the room, only light. The light was so bright and white that it hurt my eyes. I realized then that I was inside this flood of pure light, I was in awe, my spirit, my soul, my very being was separated from my shell, and the body lying so still in the bed below was mine.

I forced myself to look down again, The Chaplain was no longer holding my hand, but Her head was against the top of mine, although, my body could not feel Her, my ears could no longer hear Her words, and my spirit was aware that She was still praying for me.

I could see the top of Her head, the soft brown waves of Her hair shook as She wept for me. My skin was so pale, my body so still, from my position at the top of the room, I could hear nothing of what was going on below, and I could see perfectly. The tops of the machines, the tops of peoples heads, the backs of those bent over my body, but no faces, and I looked briefly at my own face. It didn't look like me anymore. There was no life in my face, no sparkle, the real me was no longer there, and yet, I didn't feel sad anymore.

My mind was not worried, my body felt no pain, and I knew it was over. I was calm.

The light was an ocean, I was right on the edge of it, it was like the fluffiest cloud I'd ever seen, made only of brightly glowing light, no colors, and the purest white imaginable. I was warm and comfortable.

Somehow, I knew It was okay to embrace this light, I wasn't afraid, it felt like a nurturing kind of love, and after a while, I looked back down at my shell, I could hear the thoughts of my spirit as if the words were being spoken a load, " I just want to say goodbye to my husband, and babies!". That was the last thing I remembered.

The next thing I knew, I was in a different room, Several hours had passed, and I had regained consciousness. My body had been cleaned and I had on a fresh hospital gown.

I opened my eyes, saw a Corpsman putting a bag of blood on the IV pole, He said, "Welcome Back!, You lost a lot of blood, and I was hooking up to the fifth bag of blood for your transfusion now!". I weakly said, "Gee, I hope I don't get AIDS?". The Nurse said, "That's not going to happen!", and I told Him I was only joking. He couldn't believe I had a sense of humor after everything I'd been through.

I also had intense pain throughout my body again, I had many bruises, a rash covered my skin... a reaction to the blood transfusion or the morphine shots I'd been given. My lungs throbbed, my body was weak, and I could hardly move my limbs.

My husband was at my left, but something was different, Was it me or was it Him?

Although, He was physically there for me, He seemed more distant than ever. I missed the warmth and love of the light.

I had been given "A Second Chance" at life. The life that was familiar and current. My body and my spirit were as one again, but I knew things would never be the same. I was in ICU for over three weeks, my doctors told me they didn't know how or why I survived.

It had been out of their hands and they couldn't explain my recovery. It was six months before I was fully well again and taken slowly off the Coumadin. This had been an incredible ordeal, yet, I kept to myself about what I had experienced outside of my body.

After I regained consciousness in the Hospital, I was intensely aware that for me being given back earthly life was a gift that I must be eternally thankful for. I was determined not to blow it.

I would honor God more than ever, I would listen to Him with my heart rather than my head, and I also knew that my life had not been what it should. It lacked happiness and completeness. My Marriage of four years lacked the emotional closeness I needed and this left me feeling very alone.

I started Marriage Counseling a year after being embraced by the light. I continued on and off with the counseling for the next eight years, at times I felt so alone, I was nearly suicidal, and I struggled with a weight problem for the first time in my life as well. Although, my marriage eventually ended in divorce, and I now like who I am.

My experience taught me not to fear death, It isn't scary at all, and the only fear we should have is not living the life we are given joyfully. "Life is not to be wasted!", I try to turn the negatives into positives, and keep moving forward. I never give up hope.

God Bless.

Mrs.. Jennifer L. Babb Davis

A GENTLE AFTER THOUGHT, EVERYONE IS WORTHY OF LOVE, HATE, SADNESS, HAPPINESS, AND EVERY OTHER EMOTION THAT COMES DOWN THE PIKE.

IT IS NOT UNCOMMON FOR THIS TYPE OF TRAUMATIC EXPERIENCE TO CHANGE THE PERSON WHO HAS THE EXPERIENCE, WHILE THEIR LEAVING SPOUSES AND CHILDREN UNAFFECTED. THERE IS ALSO A RATIO OF DIVORCE AMONG NDER'S (THOSE WITH NEAR-DEATH EXPERIENCE), IT IS SAD WHEN A COUPLE CAN'T COMMUNICATE FOR WHATEVER REASON.

THE DIVORCE RATIO IS: 7 OUT OF 10 WILL DIVORCE WITHIN 10YRS AFTER THE EXPERIENCE, OR SOMETIME LATER, AND IT'S HARD ON EVERYONE, NOT JUST THE NDE EXPERIENCER, BUT SPOUSES, AND THEIR CHILDREN.

MOST OFTEN, IT'S THE EXPERIENCER WHO CHANGES, THE SPOUSES HAVE TROUBLE DEALING WITH THE NEW AWARENESSES OF THE EXPERIENCER, BUT LET ME SAY THAT IT IS IMPORTANT, AND MOST VITAL, THAT THE EXPERIENCER'S COMMUNICATE WHATEVER THEY ARE FEELING. THERE IS ALWAYS SOMEONE WHO WILL LISTEN, AND THERE ARE HOTLINES IN THE SECTION OF THE PHONE BOOK.

ONE CAN NOT MAKE ASSUMPTIONS THAT THE SPOUSES ARE GOING TO UNDERSTAND, UNLESS THEY HAVE HAD THE EXPERIENCE THEMSELVES, THEY WON'T HAVE A CLUE, AND IT'S NOT FAIR TO ASSUME YOU WILL EVER GET THEM TO.

THIS IS A TRAUMATIC EVENT, THE INFORMATION YOU RECEIVE, THAT'S IF YOU RECEIVE ANY INFORMATION AT ALL, IS BASED ON THE EXPERIENCER'S LIFE, YOU MAY RECEIVE INFORMATION ABOUT OTHERS, BUT MOST OF THE TIME YOU WILL KEEP THE INFORMATION TO YOURSELF, IN FEAR OF BEING CALLED CRAZY,

OR DOCTORS MISDIAGNOSING YOU WITH SOME DISORDER YOU NEVER HEARD OF, OR SOME MAY BE FORCED WITH A MENTAL HEALTH ISSUE WITH LOTS OF STIGMA ATTACHED TO IT;

SUCH AS SCHIZOPHRENIA, BORDER LINE PERSONALITY, MANIC DEPRESSIVE, OR BIPOLAR DISORDER, SOME EXPERIENCER'S MAY EVEN TRY TO COMMIT SUICIDE, JUST TO GO BACK TO THE LIGHT, AND THE LIST CAN BE ENDLESS.

THIS BOOK HAS BEEN THROUGHLY THOUGHT OVER, REVISED MANY TIMES, BECAUSE NEW INFORMATION THAT IS ALWAYS COMIN' TO THE SURFACE, AND LET ME TELL YOU, AS AN ALTER, AN NDE CAN PUT YOU IN SUCH A TRAUMATIC SHOCK, THAT IT LITERALLY TAKES YEARS JUST FOR THE EXPERIENCER TO GET HELP, AND THE SPOUSES AND CHILDREN ARE ALONG FOR THE RIDE. (WHETHER THEY WANT TO BE OR NOT!).

THIS SECTION IS FOR INFORMATION ONLY, IT ISN'T WRITTEN IN CONCRETE OR ANYTHING LIKE THAT, IT'S JUST A GUIDE TO HOW TO GET HELP IF YOU NEED IT, AND I WOULD SUGGEST YOU TO GET HELP RIGHT AWAY, THE FIRST YEAR IS THE HARDEST.

AFFECTIONATELY, SAMANTHA, ALTER No.3

14

Spiritual Recovery & Making Peace Hanging's

Thanks to Mom, my Brothers and I were confirmed. The Sunday School programs we attended at Bethlehem Lutheran Church in East Hampton, CT are memorable. I was always close to God, that He has always been there for me, no matter what the problem was.

My Spiritual Recovery didn't come easy though, there is this thing called free will, and this often gets in the way. It's the human condition. Only now I heed the warnings and don't venture into the dark side of things.

I had a close call with what I felt was the Devil at work, it was a lesson I'll never forget, and still heed to this day. If it doesn't feel right, don't do it, and stick to what is right, don't be tempted to do the other, you may get more than what you bargin for, and the Devil is not one to take lightly.

Like drugs & alcohol, they are cunning, and powerful. If ya give it an inch, it will take more than a yard, and this is no lie.

After the auto accident of '89, I learned I had two other NDEs, the first was hellish, and the second was peaceful. I would like to talk about the hellish one for a while, you are probably wondering what it has to do with spiritual recovery, but I feel it has some very valued information to shed a light on what I call spirituality for me.

I was slipped a powerful drug at this party I had gone to, before I knew it, I was gone, It was dark, it stunk worse than death itself, and I was close to the bottom of this cliff. I was naked, stripped of modesty, hearing the moans of others around me, I was given a challenge like many others in this pit I called hell, that if I climbed to the top of this cliff I would be restored back to my original form, and not the aching misery form that I was.

Others around me had said, "Those who have done it have never come back!" I wondered what they had meant, so I prayed, and asked for help to this miserable climb.

To my astonishment, the top was much better, the stench of death no longer plagued my senses, and a voice I knew said this, "The way to Hell is short, the risks I have taken are dangerous, and long. Do not venture into the darkness anymore, that you will get more than you bargin for, this is your only warning, and to Heed it Well!".

Not knowing what to do, I prayed for forgiveness for what I had taken, that God knew it wasn't of my choosing, but to take Heed in all that I did, and I was restored to my original form.

Hours later, I went back to the Company I was assigned to, and was cautious of my actions from that time on. I felt a need to help others, I got involved with the Missionaries, and did other visits with a Cuna Tribe.

This was advised not wise, but I did it anyhow, there was an attraction I could not resist, something I couldn't explain, but I felt God watching over me, and I worked hard at compassion, peace, and understanding. To take life the Cuna offered, be wise, and be willing to learn new ways.

I wish I had read the book about the Cuna Indians before I went into the Service instead of after, because I learned about their spirituallity was more Christian than what I had learned in Sunday School, and that we had twisted religion into something that was less true, that living it, and reading it was two entirely different things.

Now I understand my first NDE, although, it was hellish, "Christ died, was sent to hell first, and was restored to the right side of the Father three days later". This is what is written in the Apostles

Creed. I truly believe those words today and everyday since that experience.

I relied on God for everything for the rest of my Tour of Duty in Panama. It hasn't been until now, that I write it in words. I believe that NDEs can be warnings or blessed gifts, something that science in any form can not dissect, there are elements I have left out to protect myself from the non-believers, that each experience is personal to the person who has the experience, and you don't have to be at death's door to have one. (An NDE that is)

To teach others about the Loving Gift of God, or whoever you may call your Higher Power, God has many names, but He knows who all His children are, to parents with children, understanding this most, you'll Love your child, no matter what that child does, and should God feel any different? "I Think Not!", but this is my own feeling, based on facts, and experience. Scientists have proved the Great Flood, yet, and many still don't believe.

Doctors, Psychiatrists, Psychologists, Pastors, Researchers, and Counselor's can put any label to anything I have experienced, from depression, schizophrenia, MPD, PTSD, and Dissociative, in the end, it's just plain survival in a World turned upside down. That Chaos is more the NORM than the truth.

That We The People are still responsible for our actions whether we accept them or not.

This is the bottom line. You can dissect that, autopsy it, twist it, bury it, repress it, but the truth will always come to the surface.

As children we are taught to tell the truth, yet some of us are still called liars, but the truth will always prevail. That Spiritual Recovery demands we speak the truth, if we lie, May the Devil Take our Souls. Spiritual Recovery is anything but easy, that it is hard work, learning can be fun, it's how we look at it, and everyone has their own ideas.

A good friend of mine from the NDE Group in Farmington has been a big help in making good suggestions when it comes to art. I have probably been dragging my feet for too long. Jack suggested that I write a paper to go with the Peace Hanging's as for how I choose the different beads, leather, and other accessories I use to decorate the wood. And why I use the type of wood that I do.

It's been a couple of years since I heard that, that now I am finally getting the energy to get it together.

At 7 Near Death Experiences, I can safely say that there is Life After Traumatic Experience. That I have been beating the odds. My faith is stronger.

Peace Hangings: A description of its meaning.
Peace Hangings are original to my own design, But the idea is taken from a Cuna Tribe Peace Offering. Which is quite different in shape, size, and purpose.

1. The round piece of pine wood is the base or grounding in which we Start from. Like Earth is our grounding.
2. The leather is to help connect all of the pieces of our lives together. Its what makes us whole in body and soul.
3. The beading is special. The colors show strength for healing. Beading also shows the colors of ones heart.
4. The feathers show the type of healing that is being asked for. Peace, forgiveness, emotional torment, and pain. The sequence for healing colors goes like this: Pink, Blue, Green, Purple, Yellow.

5. Black & White feathers symbolize dark & light sides of ones personality.

6. Other colors and types of feathers show the rank of the person in the tribe and Who they represent. Like the Chief, Shaman, or Medicine Man or Woman, Teacher Guide and Look-Outs or Protectors of the Tribe.

My own design for a Stress Reducer:
One has to find a way to keep peace in their hearts when times are stressful. Even if it's only for a few moments.

1. The round leather disc is the center or base. They come in the healing colors, grays, browns, blacks, greens, reds, and whites. (It's a custom to ask what colors the person receiving the Stress Reducer likes).

2. The Black & White braided waxed cord are used to hang the three bells and the hanger piece.

3. Smaller feathers are from indoor pet birds and feathers from craft stores. (Un-Diseased)

4. Beads & Shapes of beads are also determined by person receiving the Stress Reducer.

There's something I really would like to know, How do you generate a clinical NDE in a Laboratory? An English Psychologist has claimed to have had one, I wonder if she could explain how she pulled this off, and I would be interested in reading how this occurred. I have seen many incredible things in my life, yet, these things I have written are only true to me, and those who know me.

15

Stories from Others

Disclaimer: The views or opinions may or may not be shared by the Writer or Publishers of this book, it is others stories, and their experiences, strengths, and hopes.

I RECKON THAT ALTER PERSONALITIES CAN FALL UNDER THE TOPIC OF STORIES FROM OTHERS.

BEIN' THAT CYNTHIA IS ALREADY INTEGRATED, YA WON'T BE GETTIN' ANY STORY OUT OF HER IN PRINT, EXCEPT WHAT SHE HAS WRITTEN PRIOR TO HER INTEGRATION.

BEIN' SAMANTHA ON ANOTHER HAND, I HAVN'T QUITE FINISHED THIS TASK OF INTEGRATION. I HAVE TO SAY, "BEIN' AN ALTER PERSONALITY HAS HAD IT'S PROS & CONS. ALTHOUGH, I FEEL MOSTLY PROS.

I HAVN'T ALWAYS TOOK RESPONSIBILITY FOR MY ACTIONS, WHICH HAS PROBABLY BEEN THE BIGGEST CON OF ALL. MY TIME IN THE U.S. ARMY GOES WITHOUT SAYIN' THE TROUBLE I FOUND MYSELF IN IS ASTRONOMICAL. FOR THE MOST PART, WE GOT A VERY WISE UNDERSTANDIN' OF WHAT LIFE IS REALLY ABOUT, AND WE RESPECT OTHERS MORE FOR IT.

YOU PROBABLY THOUGHT I WOULD GO OFF WITH THIS BIG ADVENTUROUS STORY, ON THE CONTRARY, BECAUSE THERE IS ALSO A LOT I CAN'T REMEMBER EITHER, AND HAVIN' A TBI EFFECTED US ALTERS AS WELL AS OUR HOST, LAURA.

I SUPPOSE IT DOESN'T GO WITHOUT SAYIN', "IT MIGHT BE THAT MERICAL IN DISGUISE!", THAT MAY BE IT ISN'T MEANT TO BE REVEALED FOR WHATEVER REASON, AND I WILL HONOR THAT WITH A CLOSURE ON MY PART. IT'S BEEN AN EXPERIENCE TO BE HAD.

A story from Devon Stallard:

Mr. Stallard's answer to an e-mail I had received from another Source, I was very impressed by this gentlemen's response, and I did appreciate the honesty & openness.

Mr. Stallard is from New Zealand, with whom he thought I was at first. Yet, after reading the return address realized I was from the U.S.A.

Mr. Stallard writes. From waking up in Tauranga Hospital. Then thinking I was back in Nelson where I had come from in Tauranga in 1974, the accident happened on 1st April 1978. I had lived in Tauranga two years 1974 & '75, then Auckland 1976, Christchurch 1977, and part of '78. The University years at Auckland & Canterbury Universities, that is!

Now I do not remember thinking I was in Nelson I was told this latter, In fact the several Months I was in Tauranga Hospital I can not really remember and the month in Christchurch not at all of course!

My parents where told by a Neurosurgeon that I could end up a vegetable so although I was unable to finish my Law Degree and am not 100% physically. I certainly am out of the wheelchair and can almost run now!

So have done quite well. The books with people I met just here in Tauranga, population in overall area over 100,000 I believe many more books could be written, especially when one is both hearing and seeing it happen in front of ones very eyes.

People losing everything, one man two farms, then his wife, but he ensured that he provided for his four children. Two of whom are in their 20's and millionaires. So the "Brains" that their father had before the "Accident" has been handed on!

In our dictionary, brain means 1. The mass of nerve matter within the skull, the centre of consciousness and of all bodily functions. Rather a large definition.

I do have The Nelson Stallard Family Tree but can not actually remember how many Great Grandfather's William goes back. I am alive to talk about it. I was dead of course as a result of my accident but two Nurse's going by did CPR and here I am!

I have tried to lead my life as I was the Law Degree but the TBI has stopped this etc. Mr. Stallard said he would provide some names of some women who could probably answer more of the personal questions that he could not being a man.

And a Gentleman he was.

Mr. Stallard also mentioned the effects of being used by others, willingly or unwillingly giving up one's life controls and responsibilities. Mr. Stallard mentioned that as a result of his TBI, had become an epileptic with seizures after ten years of his head injury, but a doctor found the correct medication, do not have seizures since, but just can not give blood. Mr.Stallard has found that people with TBI seem to be more open and talkative.

The Near-Death Experience Paper: Death & Dying

Lecturer; Professor R. Glynn Owens

As Written by Student: Y.T. Cooper

I am only putting the NDE Story here & the rest isn't applicable at this time.

Upon mentioning to a colleague at University that I was doing some research into near-death experiences I was immediately given a paper describing a particular experience of one of our senior lecturers, psychologist Dr. Cleve Barlow. Inspired by his account and the similarity of it's content to the many NDE stories I had read up until then, I approached Dr. Barlow and asked him if I could include it in this book.

In June, 1992, Dr. Barlow suffered a sub-arachnoid hemorrhage in the brain and had to undergo neurosurgery. Due to the seriousness of his condition, Dr. Barlow's family were informed that his chances of pulling through were very slight and that they should be prepared for the worst. Dr. Barlow eventually did pull through and was released from hospital about a month after his admission. For Dr. Barlow, the time in between having the hemorrhage and a few days before leaving the hospital, almost a month, was a complete blank with exception of what he believes was an out of body and near-death experience.

"....While I was being operated on I became aware that I was suspended close to the ceiling in and out stretched horizontal position gazing down at my physical body and those who were operating on me. I stayed there for a short time and then decided to explore my surroundings. I remember floating out of the room and entering what seemed to be a long dark tunnel or some such enclosure. When I came out of the tunnel I was standing on the deck of a small cabin boat which was heading downstream. The boat was starting to negotiate a bend in the river when I observed two men dressed in white and standing on the bank to my right. Immediately, I recognized one of the men. He was Alan Patterson who died about five years ago. The boat pulled over to the embankment and I was able to greet my friend and his companion. I told them I was a stranger in these parts and I asked if they wouldn't mind showing me around. Alan replied, "that will be no trouble Cleve, this is part of our job", and they came aboard. We proceeded down stream: the river was flanked with trees and meadows.

Before long we came to a landing where we got off.

We began walking across a large rolling meadow which was dotted with clusters of trees around the edges. Then I noticed a group of people working among the shrubs and flowers off to our left and a cluster of buildings not too far from the working party. The group was about two hundred yards away from us and when we were about fifty yards from them I recognized one of the women in the group. She was Shirley Taimihinga Potaka, a colleague from university, who had passed away only three weeks or so before I went into hospital. She seemed to have recognized me too and we began waving excitedly to each other. When it became apparent to me that we weren't going to go towards the working party I said to my two friends to wait a minute that I knew someone in the group.

Shirley and I ran up to each other and kissed and embraced. I then noticed my two friends had vanished "Shirley", I inquired. "Did you see my two guides that brought me here?" "What two guides?" she replied rather sharply. "You came here by yourself". And looking very suspiciously at me she puts her hands on her hips and ordered me saying, "Cleve Barlow, you just jolly well get back to where you came from. You're not supposed to be here. You have lots to do. You haven't finished your work yet. Go on, get out of here!"

By now I was feeling more than a little embarrassed because Shirley's friends began to gather around wandering what all the commotion was about. I crept away hiding behind flowers and shrubs. I made my way back towards where we had left the boat earlier. After a time I found myself floating back into the hospital theatre. I looked down at my body lying on the operating table. Then I thought to myself, "I'd better hurry up and get back inside or I might be stranded out here". I descended onto my body and immersed myself inside....." Dr. Barlow emphasized that as far as he was concerned, this was a very real experience.

16

A Warning About the Dark Side: Intrigue & Mystery

This has been a hard chapter, because of it's contents, and what it was to be on the dark side of life. Many people i.e., are fascinated about the dark side or that hell really doesn't exist, and in my own personal journey, hell does exist. There is nothing flattering about the place, it's horrible, it stinks, and most of all, it's to noisy.

Through much of my tour of duty in the U.S. ARMY, it was stressful, a physical & mental challenge, and a spiritual challenge as well. Many people have a wide range of beliefs, which everyone shared to the extreme sometimes, which is okay for the person who had the same beliefs, but if you didn't share the same view, it became difficult to work around, and that bothered me.

Laura was told many times from a strict Roman Catholic Grandmother, she would burn in hell for not following her baptism call. That wasn't something we took lightly, but a week before she died, we talked about Heaven & Hell, that because we weren't following our baptism call we would go to hell, and I guess we would meet her down there. Gramma was quite taken back by that statement, I told her that we basically practiced the same Bible Teachings, and by her judgmental comments would definitely not put her in a good favor with the God of our understanding. Gramma apologized for not being understanding, I apologized for being so harsh, straight forward, and blunt to the point. And we made our peace. She died a week later. It made me sad to see her go, but she suffered much the past five years before her death, and I was glad that she wouldn't be suffering anymore.

Sometimes we put ourselves through hell, which is unlike the place we visited five years before, and there is quite a big difference. Only that it wasn't permanent, but a message to change our life style or that is where we would surely land up, and for that brief visit, we did make changes that would affect our direction at our death. Cynthia. Alter No. 2

It's not a place I wanted to ever see again, which brings me to this chapter, and that I am in no way going to paint a pretty picture of a place that definitely doesn't come close to pretty at all.

As Tinjcia, I have very strong feelings about Laura's role in Panama, I came to be a couple years before we went into the Service, and I am more than glad that I was able to help Laura through that hell down there. I don't share much, but this is one area that I really feel is difficult for all us personalities, including Laura.

When we went to Polland after getting out of the Service, Laura's Aunt Stasia took Her to Auschwitz-Birkenau, which I could smell fifty miles before we arrived, our Aunt wasn't convinced of that, but She hasn't been in some of the places we have been.

I am sure she has seen a lot, I will not be as so bold to say she is wrong, we all have our own hell's we have been through, real or imagined, there is not much difference. They are still traumatic, we took a few pictures, only because it was hard to believe we were actually there, and all I read in school through History books only confirmed our horror.

Our Uncle Mitch was one of the first Battalions to have liberated the prisoners, or whatever was left of them, and felt they should have leveled the place after everyone was taken out of there.

The Polish Government wouldn't let them, they turned it into a museum, and anyone under 13years of age isn't allowed. It was quite an experience, our cousins almost had to carry us out, and said, "I didn't get my color back until the evening time!". They said, " I was beyond white, more of a grayish color!".

It wasn't known at the time that us alters even existed, and I wasn't about to say anything to the contrary, it was a difficult time for us. I would not doubt the cousins on that, but we didn't go through anymore concentration camps the rest of my stay. Actually, Laura's cousins forbid to take her there unless she really wanted to go, and Laura wasn't in any shape to do that.

The camp was done okay, it was just our own perception that horrorified us, and all that we knew about the place. I did see a lot of action in the Service, it has been a hard adjustment just the same. Much is printed about the dark side, made glamorous, tempting, intriguing, and yet I am not one to test the gift that God has given me, by going into places that I know are trouble. (As we had done in the past).

The dark side is mysterious, but not to the point I would sell my soul for, and that I say most adamantly. It's not worth fame, star lights, or money, and I feel this is where I stand. I had been given drugs without consent, been stalked by men of power, and control.

They will have only one to answer to and that is not me. I did some heavy drinking, and maybe that was the reason our Higher Power felt it was time to shake us back into the real world.

I have enclosed a picture of what we saw on our trip to hell, how we got there isn't as important as the message we received, which was to change or be forever in a firey hell for the rest of our days.

It didn't take much convincing to change our attitude. It also made us wonder about those who were already there before us to spend an eternity in hell wouldn't be a picnic, the Bible talks about hell, that is where Jesus spent some time before being raised, and I can only guess why. Maybe to give those already down there a last chance for redemption? It's anyone's guess I suppose.

It wasn't until after our 3rd Near Death Experience that Laura even knew about the first & second. The second NDE was much more peaceful, which brought us to the question of why we keep being sent back on Earth. We felt somewhat rejected, than we realized our relationship with our Higher Power, God, wasn't quite what we would have liked it to be.

It's been close to 16 years since that third NDE that changed our lives, perspectives, and all that we were taught. The version of God's way hasn't been practiced for many years, isn't quite working out to His plan, or whichever Higher Power you may believe in.

As I look at all the chaos, shootings, fires, auto accidents, corruption, whatever power or control issue that comes about, it really is a sad sight, and it isn't going to get easier.

We saw a group of children who were trained to kill, it was suppose to be a Bible Camp, that isn't true, it's very easy to take a life, but it is much harder to give birth, we were suppose to be peaceful, caring people, and there are very few children being born without birth defects. Why? that isn't to hard to figure out, greed, power, control, substance abuse, no value to life, hate, revenge, only revenge is suppose to be God's judgment, and not our own.

Learning forgiveness is hard, learning to trust is even harder, being there for someone else just isn't happening to much these days, and how is it suppose to change, if no one is taking responsibility for themselves. No one is willing to stand up and admit their wrong, they pass the buck onto someone else, the children are suffering for mistakes they aren't old enough to make, and when does it stop? It stops with every individual who says, "No!", who doesn't want things to continue like business as usual The devil does temp us all of the time, that is his or her job, and when do we say, "NO!".

You could have all the money, diamonds, power, and control that you feel you need. Only there is a heavy price to be paid, your soul, and how do you get it back after the bad deed has been done? There doesn't have to be all this killing.

Life is what we make it, before you start blaming others, look at your life, and you will see you aren't far from that forbidden fruit yourself. We are no exception, I know the things we have done, being a multiple doesn't exempt us from responsibility, or accountability. When it comes to the day of facing the Higher Power, who we call God, we will have to answer to our wrong doings like everyone else.

Don't think that just because someone may claim reason of insanity to a killing or other deeds not valuing life is getting off scott-free, mental institutions are just as bad, sometimes worse than prison, and that is a fact.

Have you ever wondered why there have been so many horror movies made?, books?, and so on? Some promote evil, some let you know what the dark side is all about, glamorize, warn, and yet, how many are still watching these type of movies? Millions, myself included, and why? Because I want to learn how to not get caught up in the occults, to learn what the warning signs are, and how to avoid the actual situation from occurring. It's one more of my defects and an insatiable fascination.

We have read parts of the book Dante', seen the illustrations, and I wasn't able to finish it. It was to emotionally disturbing, the illustrations aren't off the mark, actually, they were the truth. Only in a book, you can only imagine what it smelt like, the actual feelings of living in hell didn't make us feel to great.

Which brings us to conclude, that evil is not glamorous, it's baffling, cunning, tempting, the devil will always get his or her way, and Why you may ask yourself?, because the devil has no specific rules to go by, and if you relinquish your soul, there is only one who can give it back to you.

Living the fast life is easier than living the good life. With the exception of how you get what you want from getting what you need. There is a difference, people will tell you what you need, but you're the only one who can say what you truly want.

There are always options & choices, it's up to you to do what is right for you, but don't go along with others to just be part of a pack, weigh out all possibilities of what trouble you can get into, decide if what you are doing can hurt you or others, and don't act when in question.

The old saying, "Haste makes Waste!", is in turn the truth, and if you are questioning what you are doing, then that is all the reason to not do it. With the exception of being held without your consent at gun point, knife point or other life threatening situations.

Yes, we have experienced that to.

You hold the final decision, stand on your two feet, and stay persistent. Standing confident, holding your ground, not letting on that you are afraid, even if you are, don't ever give up your ace card, unless it is a clear & present danger, that you have back-up & the support of others who can help you, and that you are all clear on what's wrong or right at the time.

I am part of Laura, as she is part of all of us, she is the host, she does have the knowledge, and awareness to stay functional. Laura has been doing it for years.

As Tinjcia, I am well educated, I share what knowledge I have if it is asked for, I don't volunteer information I don't wish to. There are areas of experience that Laura hasn't fully integrated, that would be a total shock if given all at one time, this is one of the reasons integration can take a while, and the emotions I hold must be given out moderately.

Laura has taken the courage to know how to change her life so she can have a life. It is difficult to be an alter, as it would be to be the host, and the Journey a Challenge. I will do what I can to make it less painful. Tinjcia Alter No. 4

As the teachings from the Bible says, "You can not serve two masters at one time!", a decision has to be made to serve one or the other, and there is no middle ground.

We have been to many places, done many things, and trying to keep this integration in some kind of perspective. All of what I wrote is expressed in much sadness, to lose time, having black outs or not being able to account for time is very scary, yet we have a family to raise, and I feel this is Laura's greatest accomplishment. We all have our missions in this life, one is no more important than the other, and we want to get back to the basics.

We were born to be one with each other, there were rules, and they got broken. The kids know what is happening, growing older is actually undoing what we already know that's true, we listen to the lies, and still do nothing to stop it. My theory is, when we reach the age where we want what is right, we become children again, the body is only a shell to who we really are, it's how we take care of it that makes the difference, and to nourish the soul. You can't change the past, but you can change your attitude about the past you have lived, and change is what you make of it, not what others expect of you.

The challenge in this life isn't being evil, it's being good. Doing the right thing. "Listen to the Children", is a theme in one woman's journey into being whole to herself, and family. By Shelly, et al. Thank you for being a great motivator in our search to becoming whole.

You truly helped in that process of first discovery. With much Love and Gratitude,

As Rosie, I came after the auto-accident of '89, my main mission was to put order to what was total chaos, and to be the strength to keep Laura in the teachings of what she learned in Sunday Bible School. I was also the strong force to keeping her soul intact.

As an ex-nun, I enriched her life with Music & Song, keeping her in the present, guarding against the mischief of the other alter personalities, and helping her reach inside herself to find the good things in all circumstances of her life. Good & Bad.

Keep the wind to your back & a smile on your face. Keep Peace in your Heart! Rosie

THEN THERE IS ME, SAM. I HAVE BEEN AROUND FOR QUITE A WHILE, NO STRANGER TO THE DARK SIDE OF THIS LIFE, WITH SOME REGRETS, AND A BROKEN HEART. YA MIGHT SAY THAT THE DARK SIDE HELPED BRIN' ME BACK TO MY SENSES.

I AM RESPONSIBLE FOR THAT HELLISH FIRST NEAR DEATH EXPERIENCE, WITH SOME HELP OF DRUGS & ALCOHOL, ALTHOUGH, I DIDN'T REALIZE THE TROUBLE I WAS IN UNTIL IT WAS TOO LATE.

I DIDN'T KNOW ABOUT THE DRUGS SLIPPED IN THE DRINKS I WAS DRINKIN', I KNEW I WAS IN TROUBLE, BEIN' I KNEW HOW MUCH WAS MY TOLERANCE FOR DRINKIN', AND THREE BEERS WERE WAY UNDER WHAT I WAS USE TO DRINKIN'.

I WAS TOLD THAT I KNOCKED OUT FOUR GRUNTS BEFORE I PASSED OUT.

DON'T REMEMBER WHAT IT WAS ABOUT, BUT THE BARTENDER TOLD ME LATER THAT MY PUNCHES WERE LESS THAN WHAT I WOULD HAVE DONE TO THEM NORMALLY.

I DIDN'T FIND THIS OUT UNTIL ABOUT SIX MONTHS LATER, DON'T KNOW HOW LONG I WAS GONE FOR, ALL I COULD REMEMBER WAS THIS SMELL OF BURNT

FLESH, NOW IF THAT DON'T MAKE THE HAIRS ON THE BACK OF YA NECK STAND UP, THE EXPERIENCE OF BEIN' IN HELL IS QUITE TRAUMATIC, AND WHEN WE DID FINALLY GET BACK FROM THIS EXPERIENCE, WE LEARNED THAT WE COULDN'T TRUST ANYONE.

ALTHOUGH, LAURA DID MAKE A COUPLE EXCEPTIONS, AND ENDED UP ON THE PSYCHO WARD.

THEY CLEARLY HAD AN AGENDA OF THEIR OWN, BIOFEEDBACK IS GOOD FOR RELAXATION, BUT ADDING CONTORLED SUBSTANCES TO THAT, AND ALL HELL BREAKS.

IT IS CLEAR THAT I BECAME A GOOD EXAMPLE OF THAT, A FRIEND OF MINE, ONE WHO ACTIN' LIKE ONE TOLD ME A FEW TIMES IN GROUP I BECAME SO MAD, THEY NEEDED A FEW EXTRA HANDS TO KEEP US DOWN, AND THEY KNEW ABOUT MY CIVIL SERVICE JOBS ON THE SIDE, NONE IN WHICH I TOOK ANY MONEY, I SIGNED EVERYTHIN' OVER TO A CHARITY OF MY CHOICE, BUT COULDN'T SEE WHY OTHERS COULDN'T GET SOME HELP, AND SOMETIMES THE MONIES WENT TO BUYIN' SUPPLIES TO A CUNA TRIBE IN THE DARIEN WHO I BECAME VERY CLOSE TO.

THE DARK SIDE OF THIS, WAS ALL THE DRUG TRAFFICIN' THAT WENT ON, I RECKON WE KNEW TOO MUCH, AND WAS PUT ON SOMEONE'S HIT LIST.

THAT ENDED MY CIVIL SERVICE WORK, WENT ON TO BEIN' A SPOOK.

AND NO, THAT IS ONE JOB I CAN'T EVER GIVE ANY DETAILS TO. I WOULD SAY, THAT WAS ONE OF MY BIGGEST REGRETS, BUT IN SOME WAYS, IT DID GIVE ME THE OPPORTUNITY TO HELP OTHERS WHO REALLY NEEDED THE HELP, AND WITH NO STRIN'S ATTACHED. IT SEEMED LIKE EVERYTIME I GOT CLOSE TO CERTAIN PEOPLE, I ALWAYS LANDED UP GETTIN' HURT, OR SOMEONE ELSE WOULD BE PUT

AT RISK, AND I GUESS THAT IS WHEN WE REALIZED THAT THIS TERM "FRIENDS, WAS JUST A BAD JOKE.

I WORKED MUCH OVERTIME TO KEEP LAURA AFLOAT, CYNTHIA, AND TINJCIA WERE ALSO THERE TO HELP IN THIS TOUR OF DUTY. LAURA LITERALLY SIGNED HER LIFE AWAY WHEN SHE JOINED THE SERVICE TO DEFEND HER COUNTRY.

THAT WEARIN' COLORS FOR LAURA IS A WHOLE DIFFERENT MEANIN', TO WATCH MOVIES ABOUT SERVICE ISSUES JUST AREN'T A MOVIE TO JUST ENJOY, SHE GETS WRAPPED UP IN ALL THE FEELIN'S, BETRAYAL, NOT ON THE SERVICE PART, BUT THOSE WHO WORKED WITH HER, AND THERE IS SO MUCH MORE.

I CAN SAY THAT LAURA LEARNED A LOT ABOUT WHAT HER SHELL COULD TAKE AND COULDN'T TAKE. IN MANY WAYS, IT WAS NO DIFFERENT THEN HAVIN' BEEN IN VIETNAM. A DIFFERENT GENERATION, MANY OF THE SAME KIND OF BETRAYALS, AND SITUATIONS RELATED TO SUBSTANCE ABUSE.

I SUPPOSE I CAN SHED SOME LIGHT ON WHY MANY DIDN'T COME HOME FROM VIETNAM, IT PROBABLY TOOK ABOUT THE SAME COURAGE TO COME HOME AS TO THOSE WHO DIDN'T, AND IT IS SAD.

THOSE WHO WERE BADLY WOUNDED LANDED UP ON HEAVY DRUG MEDICATIONS, LOSS OF LIMBS, AND SO ON. THEN YOU HAVE THE ONES TAKEN PRISONER, KILLED, OR SERVERELY TREATED, AND THEN YOU HAVE THOSE WHO WERE IN AREAS THAT WERE GASSED BY AGENT ORANGE OR MUSTARD GAS. THESE CHEMICALS AREN'T SOMETHIN' YA WANT TO BRING HOME TO THE WIFE OR KIDDIES. AND LASTLY, MANY BECAME SPOOKS, THEY FELT THEY WERE DYIN' ANYWAY, MIGHT AS WELL MAKE GOOD USE OF THEIR TIME, AND TALENTS WHILE THEY WERE STILL ALIVE.

I AM SURE THERE WOULD BE A LOT TO ARGUE ABOUT, BUT ONCE YA KNOW. THERE'S NO TURNIN' BACK, YA EITHER LEAVE AND GET BACK TO LIFE, OR YA STAY BEHIND IN THE DARK.

LAURA WAS TOO FAMILY ORIENTED, THAT RUNNIN' THE REST OF HER LIFE JUST DIDN'T WORK FOR HER, AND HAVIN' BEEN PUT ON A HIT LIST JUST WASN'T SOMETHIN' SHE CONSIDERED AS AN OPTION. WITH THREE TRIES ON HER LIFE ALREADY, SHE FELT IT WOULD BE BETTER TO TAKE HER CHANCES ON THE OUTSIDE. ALTHOUGH, LAURA DID HAVE A CHATWITH THE PERSON WHO PUT HER ON THE HIT LIST, AND THEY RESOLVED THEIR ISSUES.

WE TURNED OUT OKAY, SOMETHIN'S STILL SPOOK US, CROWDS MAKE US REAL NERVOUS, AND BUSES, WE JUST DON'T USE THEM UNLESS WE REALLY HAVE TO. SOMETIMES WE JUST DON'T FEEL WE BELONG. DAVE IS LAURA'S LIFE SAVER, THE LAST CHANCE SHE COULD PROVE THAT SHE COULD RAISE A FAMILY, AND BLEND INTO THE WOODWORK. (WOODWORK, MEANIN' THE TRADITIONAL FAMILY LIFE).

AS LAURA'S THERAPIST PUTS IT, WE HAVE TOO MANY BAD ANNIVERSARIES THAT HAVEN'T BEEN PUT BEHIND US, TO JOGGLE WITH ON A DAILY BASIS, WE WILL TAKE ONE AT A TIME, AND GET SOME CLOSURE ON THEM BEFORE THEY MAKE US REALLY CRAZY.

FOR LAURA, ET AL. TO COME OUT OF THE CLOSET, IS A BIG LEAP IN RISK TAKIN', THAT SHE DOESN'T HAVE TO STAY ON THE DARK SIDE, AND THAT SHE IS WORKIN' HARD TO TALK ABOUT THE BETTER THIN'S LIFE HAS TO OFFER.

IT DOESN'T MEAN SHE WILL FORGET THE PAST, BUT THAT SHE HAS THE COURAGE TO SHARE WITH OTHERS, HER EXPERIENCE, STRENGTHS, AND HOPE'S.

THAT THE PEOPLE SHE COMES IN CONTACT WITH HER WILL KNOW THERE ARE OPTIONS & CHOICES AVAILABLE TO THOSE WHO SEEK THE TRUTH IN THEMSELVES.

IT HAS BEEN AN INTERESTIN' LIFE, IN A WAY, THIS BOOK HELPS PUT CLOSURE ON A PAST SO FRAGMENTED, PUTTIN' THE PIECES TOGETHER, AND NOT GIVIN' UP.

AFFECTIONALLY,
SAMANTHA

I reckon it's my turn to add to this dark side of thin's. Yes, it has been dark indeed. Two suicide attempts, all failed of course. I suppose I really didn't want to die, but go back to the light we experienced in the '89 auto accident.

Our lives were changed dramatically from that day on, unlike the other two NDE's before, this one really affected every part of our soul, and it was so peaceful.

I supposed we got scrambled when Laura's head went through the drivers side window, not rememberin' to much that is clear, except the NDE itself, and that is as clear as day.

One of the best thin's that Laura did was to go to get clean & sober, which She did from the back door like so many others her age, and learned that there is life after addiction.

Laura was just over a year when the '89 crash occurred, that helped Her stay focused, and out of trouble for the most. Laura didn't have far to go to get into trouble, it followed her everywhere.

I am not quite sure what brought me to think I could commit suicide, it wasn't somethin' I could describe, but it didn't happen, I guess Laura's Angels have been workin' triple time or somethin' like that, and I suppose that is past issue stuff.

But what could make someone take their own lives?, definitely not sanity, far from it, and knowin' the type of gal that Laura is, not somethin' intentionally that is.

I guess despair is a drivin' force, low self-esteem, escape from long term abuse, not necessarily physical, but emotional and mental torture qualifies in the scenario, and knowin' somethin' bad had happened, but can't figure it out.

Laura was asked out on a date when She worked as a CNA, just before goin' into the ARMY, She was at Friendly's, was one of her summer night spots after a long day at work, How bad could this guy be?, we weren't in a bar, it seemed a safe thin' to do, and so Laura agreed to meet Him for a Church Function.

Looks were definitely deceivin' that evening, Laura landed up runnin' from that church after watchin' a plant she poured her drink on, die, that wasn't just soda in that cup, and made an excuse to be excused. When She got to the corner of the street block, She nearly ran into a Policeman, This Officer asked why we were runnin'?, and did I need assistance?, We were to out of breath to say, but that if a man came runnin' after me, to stop him, so she could get away, and when she got home, shut the door, ran to the bedroom, shut that door, took out the Bible to read the verses she had copied from the Church she had attended, and she was just glad she was finally home. Some time had passed, Dad made Mom check to see what had happened, when we told Mom what had happened, Mom just hugged Her, and told Laura that a hot bath may calm Her down. She had gone back to Friendly's a week later, this man hadn't come back since the week before, and I guess ya could say we felt safer.

One of Laura's cousins did join the occult for sometime, but had taken suggestions of checkin' out a few thin's, and left. My cousin changed phone numbers, and didn't live back at home. I reckon she didn't want anyone goin' to her parents home and causin' harm to anyone.

After much research on the occult, I respect their belief of what they are, but if I don't personally share the same views, I don't want to be hassled. My spiritual belief's are my own, I share only when asked, and I don't hassle anyone about their own.

We saw Laura's Dad rip his Mom up one side and down the other for her jokin' about a Jehovah's Witness that came to the door, we had never seen Dad act like that, and said, "That one doesn't ever joke about someone else's religion!". Kindly say, "No Thank You!", and close the door.

There are religions that do put out a false front to reel you in, but if somethin' sounds to good to be true, your first instinct should be a cautious one, and report to your resident trooper about your concerns. If ya have any concerns that is.

I reckon that some organizations do go to extremes, don't just ignore threats, report them. When in question, tell them ya think it over, and if ya interested, have them give ya their number in case ya want to reach them.

I reckon I've said enough about what can happen, brainwashin', wipe-out bank accounts, turn family members against one another, and the list goes on. There are the occults that do none of which has been mentioned, and are quiet, peaceful members of society.

I am not sure about some of the programs on TV that address the dark side, we all have a dark and light side, we are capable of both, if ya say that is not true, ya only foolin' ya self, and not bein' true to who ya are. Given the right circumstances, situations, and substances, one could land up doin' just about anythin'.

Another clue to dark side behavior, doin' thin's that make ya withdraw or isolate, if ya a sociable individual, also can be a clue to drug abuse, and loud acid rock. There is a story to every sung written, some are just clearer than others, and most do come from the heart.

Just make sure ya not hurtin' ya self or others. (This does include animals). If ya doin' somethin' that hurts ya or others, get help, the issue may be much bigger than what ya aware of, and it's easier to get to the source if others are involved workin' for ya not against ya.

Certain Cartoon shows are questionable, screen what ya kids be watchin', it does make an impression that ya as a parent might not be aware of, and it does matter to them when ya actively checkin' on progress they make at school. Stay involved!

Be good to ya self, keep a peaceful heart,

Cynthia

I guess it's my turn as the Host of all these others, I am just learning more about what my alters have done for me, I never had a clue, growing up I was called a space cadet, air head, and sometimes dizzy blonde.

To live six different life styles in one body is quite incredible, yet, I feel in some way, they knew what they were doing even if I did not. That is what has given me the most courage.

My Husband, Dave really had a better insight than I did, and it's hard to see things objectively when you're right in the middle of things.

Dave talked about past lives all the time, I really didn't see the light until I woke up one morning with bruises on my forearms, Dave did tell me how I got them, and I didn't remember. That was the real shocker for me, I did get help, and I was glad for His honesty.

Dave was the only one who I really spent a consistent time with. We just thought we were living in some kind of hell we couldn't escape from, you really can't run away from who you are, you can try escaping, but the bottom line is, it is always you who is in the mirror, and it doesn't matter what name you call yourself, it's always you.

With all the horror movies I have watched, most were for fun, but in my last 9yrs., they are no longer fun to watch, I still watch them from time to time, but they hold a different meaning for me today, and some I can still laugh at, but most make me sad, and depressed.

The psycho dramas are just to real to watch, the shows like: Forever Knight, Buffy the Vampire Slayer, Outer Limits, and even X-Files get to hard to watch at times. Poltergeist, the Legacy, and Highlander is more our speed, and the fight against evil is to fascinating not to watch. It sort of gives me an inside track as what to stay away from in the real world.

That some of these History Channel shows about, ancient times, mysteries, and facts of the Bible bring still a lot of questions. I don't believe in disturbing sacred burial grounds to see what they died of, several excavations in the eastern parts of the world like, Africa, Indonesia, South, Central, and Eastern parts of the U.S.A. are transmitting diseases that should not have been excavated. Although, there are some disease's that are produced in nature that are unknowns.

I love Science and History, but I doubt I would want to go to any of the excavation sites of which some diseases have been retransmitted because of bodies excavated, and one thing that Dad always instilled in us as kids was to never say anything ill-willed about the dead, and to respect the grounds in which people are laid to rest.

Now-a-days the vandalism of Cemeteries is definitely an evil malicious act, or drug & alcohol related act, sometimes they are occult related, and whatever the case, something's are to just be left alone. My own opinion.

It's not hard to tell wether something's are right or wrong, moral values have changed drastically, and what used to be un-tolerated in society, is now being tolerated.

The dark side is everything that is done in darkness and the light side is everything done in the light, this is not always the case, that there are equal amounts of both done on both sides.

Bad things that happen to good people and good things happen to bad people, this is in general of course.

There are both sides of the self. The Ying & The Yang, good & bad, Darkness & Light, right or wrong, we are all capable of both, and that is the balance of who we are. Abusive & bad upbringing isn't an excuse for bad behavior, neither is good upbringing an excuse for bad behavior.

It is written that all sin was the same in God's Eye's, Whether it was stealing or murder, there was a punishment to fit the crime, and in modern days, "If you can't do the time, don't do the crime!", a quote taken from the TV show Beretta. (Tony Blake starred in).

One mistake can be accepted as ignorance, a second mistake to the same deed is a definite wrong, and ignorance can't be used as an excuse. Once it is put in your awareness, you have to act or not act, you always have a choice, you don't always have an option.

The dark & light sides will always be opposites, you have to acknowledge they both exist, you have the option to act or not act on either side, and the choice is up to you?

My Higher Power is God, to everyone else reading this, it is whoever your Higher Power is to you, it is not for me to say or debate over, and respect to that is always given.

Here are a few books that might help a parent, sibling, or friend to recognize when they feel a person close to them might be in serious trouble, and what can be done to prevent injuries to self or others.

BEYOND THE DARKNESS My Near-Death Journey To The Edge of Hell And Back Angie Fenimore Foreword by Betty J. Eadie

A Probing Analysis of The Newest Religious Craze **THE NEW AGE RAGE** By Karen Hoyt And The Spiritual Counterfeits Project

GLOBAL PEACE AND THE RISE OF ANTICHRIST by Dave Hunt

Beyond The Light: The Mysteries and Revelations of Near-Death Experiences by P.M.H. Atwater

A Reason to Live by Melody Beattie

AMERICA THE SORCERER'S NEW APPRENTICE The Rise of New Age Shamanism by Dave Hunt & T.A. McMahon

17

Head-on Crash
** No Where to Go **

It was January 24, 2001 and at11:47 A.M. Roads were dry and the day was sunny. Hardly a cloud in the sky. I was driving out of Motta's Pastry & Bake Shop, Inc. And taking a Right hand turn onto Rt. 6 in Columbia. I was going East Bound. A car coming from the other direction passed over the double yellow lines and struck my car head on.

You could say this didn't make my day. I had put a lot of money into getting the car fixed just recently, and I had planned on keeping it for a while. I was crushed emotionally. Physically, still up for debate, and having no wheels to drive around, which really sucks.

It took a few days just to find out how the other driver was. Around 86 yrs. old, yet could have been a medical condition that could have caused the accident. I really didn't want to believe I was in an accident when it happened. I recall asking one of the Police Officers if it was for real, and He said, "Sorry Ma'am, but it was true!".

The Officer said, " I could count myself as another statistic!" and I said, "How? The road didn't come up and total my car, it was another car. The famous Suicide 6, driver's use the conditions of the road on Rte. 6 to excuse bad driving, and it gets real old. Those who do choose to blame the road for accidents forget that it is people who make the roads. No One Is Perfect. As my Aunt Stasia would say, "No Such Animal!". How does one get away from a head-on crash when you are struck by a car in your lane and the guard rails with snow on the shoulders? Where is one to go? I can say that my car did it's job in saving my life, I am content with just being alive, and that no was killed.

I will say this, as a driver, driving is a privilege not a right, and that driving is taking a risk. Everyone is accountable whether they are responsible or not. Learning how to trust the circle of life is not an easy task, but it is attainable if sought out with faith and love.

A Near Death Experience again, not again, yes, and what a nightmare it turned out to be.

After over a year of pain or loss of feeling in my right shoulder down, dropping things, and just sick and tired of the feeling that something was wrong. It turned out that I was going to need surgery to remove a herniated disc in my neck, which was causing the problem.

It is a possibility that I may need surgery later down the road. I didn't realize the full extent of the neck problem myself and how severe it could turn out to be. I am on the mends and doing well for now. I pray it stays that way.

18

The Mountain Climb that Turned into a Nightmare

It was July 1, 2002. The Combs Family started hiking up Mt. Crawford. It was about 1 p.m. when they started their accent up the mountain.

It was hot but tolerable. There was a nice breeze. They even got to see one of the local snakes that inhabit the region. The twins, (Lee & Keith) were really excited about that.

The day started out cloudy, but turned to be a clear day. The trail however, was a lot rougher terrain than what was written in the guide book. At least, this is how I felt about it. I didn't complain about it though. We all reached the top, took pictures, drank lots of water going up, and enjoyed the beautiful sights. It was breezy, it felt nice on my sweaty body. The tree line was in most of the trail. It wasn't like we were in the direct sun for the trip coming down the mountain. The breeze was really refreshing. Our decent went fine considering the terrain for about the first mile and 1/2. Then it was like my legs started to hurt and not work right. Then about another 1/2 mile down, my legs were turning into jello and not wanting to work at all. I kept sitting down, falling backwards, banging my legs against rocks, and then my legs wouldn't work at all.

I knew at that point I was in serious trouble, my husband Dave got really worried. He said, "I acted like my mother when she was having a diabetic reaction!", confused, rambling on about nothing, and really out of it. The Twins were a little further down the trail and Dave needed them to get help.

It felt like it was raining for a time, I was so far away from myself, I could see what was happening, but it was like I couldn't respond, although, it was said that I was answering questions. A couple lived on Mt. Crawford. To my great luck, they were actively involved with the E.M.S. Services, and they had kids who were older, took care of our boys for the rest of the day and night. They left there name and address with the E.M.T.'s at the bottom of the Mt. I must have lost consciousness a few times along the way.

I really don't have much recall as to what was going on when or before I reached the bottom of the Mt. Then I was carried in a litter to the road where an ambulance was waiting to take me to the hospital, which turned out to be 25 miles away in North Conway.

I guess we had run out of water half way down, I was diagnosed with extreme heat exhaustion, and the CPK's (Blood platlets that can block the flow of blood to the vital organs, making the organs fail, and shut down), were at 43,000. When I asked what they are suppose to be, the doctor said, "About 54 for a woman my size!".

Dave just looked at me. It took eight days to get them down to 6,000. The Doctor (Diana Snow) was not too thrilled about me leaving with that level, but Dave had no more money for the Motel, we had the campsite only until July 4th. Not the way to spend a vacation. It took two more weeks to get the CPK's to 1,400, and another week for it to go down to 77. With none of the proteins that would pose a problem for the kidneys.

Near Death Experience or out of Body Experience? Whatever the case, it is not one in which I would like to experience again in this lifetime. Why am I writing about this, because it was very painful, and I am just starting to build my body up again so I can begin hiking again. It is a fun, relaxing, and spiritual sport. It can also kill you if you don't have everything to keep yourself safe. My Doctor

(Christopher Bentley, D.O.) said, "You can never have enough water & that is what is most important for any outside or inside sport!"

Don't let what happened to me happen to you. It is also very costly, you get charged for whatever is used to save you. I had to get down that Mt. with help, there was no way to get a chopper to me, I was too far into the tree line.

Just to give you an idea how serious my condition was, I'll give you some information to help you understand.

Rhabdomyolysis: Myoglobin is an iron-containing pigment found in the skeletal muscle. When the skeletal muscle is damaged, the myoglobin is released into the bloodstream. It is filtered out of the bloodstream by the kidneys. Myoglobin my occlude the structures of the kidney, causing damage such as acute tubular necrosis or kidney failure.

Acute tubular necrosis: Is a kidney disorder involving damage to the renal tubule cells, resulting in acute kidney failure. (ATN) is caused by ischemia of the kidneys (lack of oxygen to the tissues), or by exposure to materials that are poisonous to the kidney (nephrotoxic agents).

Ischemia and Necrosis: **a.** Reduction or absence of blood supply to an organ or tissue.

b. Etiology: Clot, atherosclerotic plaque, hypoxemic vasoconstriction.

Infarction: death of an area of tissue as a result of ischemia

Necrosis: Cells and tissues die by either necrosis or apoptosis, et al.

Acute renal failure: Acute renal failure is a sudden loss of the kidneys' ability to excrete wastes, concentrate urine, and conserve electrolytes.

These are just four things that can happen to you if you don't have enough water with you. This is not to scare you, it is information that can save your life. Or maybe someone you love, Or maybe a stranger you happen by.

As part of the human condition, some people feel this can never happen to me, they ignored the warning signs, or maybe you'll say, "Not enough water, that wasn't a smart thing!". How much is enough water?, it depends on how far you plan on hiking, the weather, and how you are feeling on the day of your trip. One of the biggest problems could be the terrain you are hiking on. And miscalculating the amount of water needed for your trip.

Those guide books are okay if you live in the region, but sometimes can be misleading to someone who may live somewhere else. Always check with the Rangers' Stations when you aren't sure about the terrain listed in the guide-book.

To clear up any assumptions that might be made, or criticisms, or judgments that may be made about my situation, it was a freak thing, and we did have water, just not enough for the trip down. Only why me and not the rest of my family? I am not going to beat myself on the head repeatedly for this. I can't change what happened, but I can make sure it doesn't happen again. It could have been any number of variables that caused what happened to me.

The recovery also took longer than expected, but I have been doing a lot of research and slowly building myself back up to hiking again in the immediate future.

I would like to Thank Nancy, Merle, and Family for all you did for my family and me, the Ambulance Crew, the great work they did to hydrate me, and to all at The Memorial Hospital, the Nursing Staff, and the Emergency Staff.

To Dr. Diana Snow, I know that you were disappointed when you would have to give the news that I couldn't go home each day you were in. I also know how reluctant you were when my CPK's were 6,000 and you still had to send me home. I am fine now. Thank You for the great care you gave me while I was at your Hospital.

It has been a strain on the boys, they don't want to hike anymore, and they blame their Dad despite all efforts to sway them into another way of thinking. We are just going to have to start hiking again when the weather gets better and have everything you are suppose to have and more. I don't see any other way to sway them into believing that what happened was an un-expected accident and that we won't let it happen again.

One day the twins may choose to write about there own experience on what happened, but for now, they no longer blame their Dad for this, and that it was just an unfortunate mishap.

In Conclusion: To All Who Read This: There Is Life After Traumatic Experience.

I have been Beating The Odds for Years. And so have so many others. May the Spirits Embrace You with Love and Happiness Always.

Laura R. Combs

19

The Mistake on Mt. Crawford
By Lee R. Combs

You will hear my story about my mountain mishap. It was very frightening, because the leaves were very slippery.
Dad sent my Brother and I down the mountain alone to get help for Mom, she wasn't doing to well, and she ran out of water. (Actually, we all ran out of water).
Although, we were in better shape than Mom was, and this could have been one of the factors that caused Mom to get into medical trouble.
Mom became so dehydrated that she suffered heat exhaustion, delirium, and was totally sick to her stomach and was vomiting in her hat. (Yes, we did leave the hat on the mountain on a rock or somewhere out of the way so others wouldn't step in it or on it).
It began to rain a little, Dad sent us down the mountain to get help. Dad stayed with Mom so nothing would happen to her.
My mishap occurred before Mom was in trouble. About half way down the mountain, I slipped on wet leaves, when my walking stick got caught on two trees. landed up lying on my stomach hanging off a land bluff 200 ft., looking down the side of the mountain.

If my walking stick didn't get caught, I would have slid down 200 ft. into some trees.

(OUCH!!!).

My brother Keith helped me up from where I had landed on the side of the mountain using his walking stick. I was more than glad I had a sibling that day.

In conclusion, I don't recommend climbing mountains in 90 degree weather without Lots of water, and make sure you are fit enough to climb after checking in at the Ranger's Station before you leave. Let others know where you are going, and when you're expected to come back. My brother Keith doesn't remember the details of this and feels he doesn't have a story to tell. This is not uncommon for some people to block out situations so traumatic to them while rescuing someone close to them.

20

The Music that Has Inspired Me & Suggested Readings for Better Understanding

There's Music that touches the Heart, a lot of the Music I was brought up with is changed for me, and that I look at it with more attention. Some music I listen to is native, not just to North America, but everywhere in everything. I have learned for myself about what issues the World is song about, violence, joy, hatred, love, fear, faith, anguish, strength, abuse, drugs, and I know for myself what is most inspiring.

All the way from classic, jazz, blues, spiritual enlightenment, rock and roll, to hard rock (Instrumentals), and elevator music as some would say.

I will list them below. Keeping in mind, what inspires me is not necessarily in the same views of the song writers or performers.

Pop Singers:	Blues & Jazz:	Native music:
Madonna	B.B. King	Solitire
Celine Dion	Stevie Ray Vaugh	Sacred Drums
Mariah Carey	Billie Holiday	Old Man Coyote

Cindi Luaper   Norah Jones   Celtic Woman

Country singer:	Rock & Roll:	Instrumentals:	Celtic Music
Reba McIntire	Fleetwood Mac	Yanni	Folk Music
Alan Jackson	Jimmy Hendrix	Mozart	Church Music
Kenny Rogers	Lynard Skinard	Bach	Native American
Kathy Mattea	Stevie Nicks	Chopin	Handbell Music

Do to having a Bipolar Disorder, Multiple Personality Disorder, PTSD from the Military and a few auto accidents, and depression from time to time. I have had time to do lots of reading and research.

Here are the books I would suggest reading:

The Dreaming Universe by Fred Alan Wolf, Ph.D.

Page 95 Unilateral Stroke

Page 101 All epileptics

The Dragons of Eden by Carl Sagan

An Unquiet Mind: A Memoir of Moods & Madness by Kay Redfield Jamison

The Broken Brain by Nancy Andreason

Coping with Emotional Disorders by Carolyn & Dwain Simpson

From Sad to Glad: Kline on Depression by Nathan S. Kline, M.D.

A Brilliant Madness: Living with Manic Depression Duke P.

Hochman G. Bantam Books, New York, 1992

Call Me Anna The Autobiography of Patty Duke Duke P. Turan K. Bantam Books, New York 1987

Depression and Antidepressants: A Guide. Sen D, Jefferson JW, Greist JH. Information Centers, Dean Foundation, Madison, WI rev. ed. 1996.

Genes and the Mind: Inheritance of Mental Illness. Tsuang MT, VanderMey R. Oxford University Press, New York, 1980

"Out on a Limb" by Shirley MAClaine

"Going Within" by Shirley MAClaine

Printed in the United States
137191LV00004B/7/P